GER McKENNA on greyhounds

John Martin

RINGPRESS

Published by Ringpress Books Limited 1989.

Spirella House, Bridge Road,
Letchworth, Herts SG6 4ET

© John Martin, 1989

Production Consultants: Landmark Ltd of London
Printed and bound in Great Britain by Redwood Burn Ltd

ISBN 0 948955 90 2

Contents

Introduction 5
Chapter One: Early Years 9
Chapter Two: Family Rivalry 18
Chapter Three: The Trainer 29
Chapter Four: Prince of Bermuda 37
Chapter Five: English Derby 53
Chapter Six: Irish Derby 71
Chapter Seven: Costello Derby 77
Chapter Eight: Irish Cesarewitch 86
Chapter Nine: Irish Laurels 94
Chapter Ten: The Racing Kennel 104
Chapter Eleven: A-Z of Practical Hints 111
Chapter Twelve: Coursing 118
Chapter Thirteen: The Waterloo Cup 124
Chapter Fourteen: The Maestro 131
Appendices
I: Breeding and Extended Pedigrees 138
II: Ger McKenna's 32 Classic Winners 146
III: Other Feature Winners 147
IV: St Leger Roll of Honour 148
V: Irish Derby Roll of Honour 149
VI: McKenna's Great Greyhounds 152
VII: Bibliography 160

Ger McKenna with Parkdown Jet, in the week before the 1981 English Derby final.

Introduction

IN the strange way that memory seems to dictate that we remember all our summers past as idyllic, I recall it as a gloriously sunny day. The mental picture is of overgrown hedgerows interwoven with flowering briars and the buzz of bumble bees. Heathrow Airport had been familiar territory and even on the train to Potters Bar I felt comfortable, surrounded by people who would direct the lost. Now in the rural outskirts of London, I was not so sure. An appreciation of the countryside soon gave way to panic. It was Friday, June 26, 1981. Late Friday. As the then newly-appointed Greyhound Correspondent of Independent Newspapers in Ireland, I had been sent to report on the fate of the three Irish-trained runners in the final of the English Derby at White City on the following evening. The least difficult task was deciding the trainer from whom I would glean some snippets of information on which to base a plausible prediction of the outcome of the race, for the following morning's newspaper. In Ireland you needed to know nothing of greyhounds to know of Ger McKenna. In the same way that every housewife knew of Lester Piggott. McKenna's affinity to the sport back home was that close. He was the sport. There was no difficulty in making my choice. But my watch ticked closer to the deadline and I seemed no nearer to finding him. Suddenly the calm of the late afternoon was shattered. Not too far in the direction in which I was heading was the sound of music, loud music, bold and brassy. At least here was someone who could possibly assist the lost and weary scribe. The door was open and there stood a small, round man.

"You wouldn't happen to know where I could find Ger McKenna, the greyhound trainer?" I ventured.

"And who might you be?" replied the man, whose Irish accent brought to me the sort of glow that a pilgrim feels when he enters the unknown and finds that he is among brethren.

"So you're Mr Martin. Come in."

This was the great Ger McKenna. The man, in Irish sporting terms on the same pedestal as John Doyle or any of the highly decorated hurling immortals of his native County Tipperary, was pottering among the tea cups, neatly stacked on a roughly cut table in the corner.

Well . . ." he said, turning to me when the tea had brewed. McKenna uses the word often. Later, you come to realise that it is: "Well, what have you got to tell me?" It takes you no time at all to get to know Ger McKenna. It takes you years to realise that you did not know him at all. I had little to tell him. We talked of people we both knew, my predecessors in the job. He was happy to talk. McKenna, too, could relax talking to one of his own. A long time later I realised why. It was now late June — he had been here in this remote spot since mid-May. Virtually alone.

His wife Josie candidly says: "I hate the English Derby. It means six weeks of separation."

Ger now recalls: "Those days before the GRA kennels at Potters Bar were disbanded were hell. The loneliness. They had a place up the way where you could have a mineral and there was a pool table. But it was not for me. In those days I found it hard to mix. Sundays were the worst. There wasn't the normal coming and going. It wasn't like home, where you could salute somebody and get into conversation with them. You could even pick an argument — give a fella a bollocking, just to liven things up."

But this was McKenna's job. Something which he must do for that dreaded six weeks of the year. Of course, there were breaks from the ennui. There was the excitement of setting out from base camp in Borrisokane, the boat across the Irish Sea. Ger McKenna is a professional. Nothing was forgotten. There was the Irish water, not that it was any clearer of impurity than the English aqua, just that it was what the dogs were used to — and there was less chance of their systems being upset. And there, stacked neatly at the back of the table, was Irish brown bread. That was for the dogs, too.

"Come on and I'll show ye this fella."

He opened the back door and the sound was almost deafening. The

Boston Pops Orchestra playing a Sousa march under Ger McKenna. I was being given a complimentary Master Class in the art of greyhound training. The Maestro at work. I was not going to go away, forever wondering why the dog with the sleek blue coat was sitting there with his ear cocked to a transistor radio.

His master's voice spoke: "It's to get him used to the crowd and all the noise tomorrow night."

Just over twenty-four hours later the same sounds filled the London air. There was an almost tangible nervous expectancy in the packed White City Stadium. The Band of Her Majesty's Royal Marines belted out the tunes as we waited anxiously for that vital time, 10.28, to come around. Only Parkdown Jet's heart was not fluttering, he must have felt very much at home. It is no exaggeration to say that the vast majority wanted Ger McKenna to win. Not Parkdown Jet, not owner Sean Barnett, but Ger McKenna. If they did not actually will him to win, then they certainly would not begrudge him doing so. Their money might have been invested on the Totalisator on some bigger-priced finalist, but it was only an interest. They really wanted Ger to win. They felt they almost knew him, they had seen his picture in *The Sporting Life* and he had been coming to White City for years. He was a vital part of Britain's greyhound racing showpiece. Nowadays, White City is spoken of in awe. Those who never stood on its terraces on a big greyhound racing night are the poorer. I am glad to have done so, even if just to appreciate what they are talking about. Some Irish trainers have never gone back since the stadium's demise. The White City was too integral a part of the English Derby. Physically, it could be transferred. But the spirit has been left behind. Apart from all else, it was a fair track, its turf painstakingly manicured by the staff, revered by racegoers; its bends sweeping and ample enough to accommodate six greyhounds at full stretch.

On that night in June 1981, Ger McKenna's pilgrimage to White City paid off. Parkdown Jet took honours in the English Derby and McKenna claimed the classic, which he confesses has become like a religion to him. When the Derby moved to Wimbledon in 1985 McKenna moved with it. It was his job to do so. It was the professional thing to do.

"If my owners want to run their dogs in the Derby at Wimbledon, then I will go," he said, when it was announced that Plough Lane was to be the new home of the Greyhound Derby. When it was suggested that others might effectively boycott the venue, he replied: "Good. It will make it easier for me to win."

Eight years later, it seemed like old times. A balmy summer's day and an unimposing collection of kennels secreted at the bottom of a narrow lane near the village of Tiddington, ten miles from Oxford.

"Well . . ." he said.

There were no need for introductions this time. It was late June, 1989.

"Owen, stick on the kettle, and higher up the radio . . ."

I was about to be told all about a black dog out the back. The Derby might not be at White City. But, tomorrow night, Ger McKenna had a runner, the favourite, in the final. The dog's name was Lartigue Note. . .

CHAPTER ONE

Early Years

EVERYONE has probably passed through Nenagh at one stage or other — passed through, but never stopped. By local standards it is a sizeable place. In Irish Gaelic it is Aonoch, meaning a fair. It is described as a town simple because, unlike the typical Irish village, it has tributaries to its main street. Its plastic signs for burger joints constitute Nenagh's only concession to modern life. Intrinsically, it has changed little from the days when it was the market. The bank, the hotel, the drapery shop, the betting office; all are located in buildings where the facade has changed little. The meat factory, aluminium plant and plate-glass factory are the main employers. But unemployment is high in Nenagh. Everyone has probably passed through at one stage or other. Because they have to. Nenagh is on the main road from Limerick to Dublin. Nenagh is the nearest centre of population to Borrisokane. Nobody passes through Borrisokane. Unless you take the wrong road out of Limerick. Geographically it is quaint — within easy reach of counties Galway, Clare, Limerick and Offaly — and yet it is in another county altogether. Borrisokane is in Tipperary, fiercely so when it comes to the day of the big hurling match. In no other way is the North Tipperary hamlet unique. It is a traditional Irish village of eight hundred souls and fourteen public houses. Of course, Borrisokane knows there is a world outside. The advent of RTE television in the early Sixties had seen to that and Nenagh is only ten miles down the road. More importantly, Ger McKenna has been going away every year with the dogs to the legendary White City and he had even won the English Derby. But life does not, generally, pass through Borrisokane. More often than not, it passes it by. That is until June 24, 1989, when Borrisokane could just as easily have been the middle of the universe, with Slevin's Electrical Shop its centre of gravity. One of the pubs had a satellite dish on order, but it had not been delivered. Slevin's was the only place that they could get Sky television and Slevin's had opened at 10.25 on a Saturday night; and the town, those who were not in London, crowded in to see the only Borrisokane man known outside Borrisokane win the English Derby with Lartigue Note.

"You're not near anywhere and yet you're central," is how Gerard McKenna, Greyhound Trainer, The Square, Borrisokane, Co. Tipperary, describes the village where on February 27, 1930, he was born, the first child of his father's second marriage. Malachy McKenna, a cattle dealer, had six brothers and thirteen children. He thus became the central figure in a family of dynastic proportions. Malachy's father's family had owned the local pub — The Greyhound Bar — which, in traditional manner, doubled as a grocery store. Malachy's mother's family had the drapery shop. The Lambes, the Ryans, the Gilfoyles who had the forge up the hill. All were relatives. "I was related to them all, if only by the buttonhole," says Ger. "My father was a cattle dealer rather than a farmer." The McKenna brothers of Malachy's generation were his older brother, Michael, and the younger Joe, Tim, Jack, Frank and Paul. All had "a dog or two", Ger recalls. But it was in another sport that the McKennas first made their name. The national game of hurling had and has always been a county and clan passion and Ger's uncle Paul was a member of a victorious Tipperary side. Ger was not six months old at the time but, today, greyhound racing is his work, hurling his passion. Paul's elder brother Joe moved to Templeogue in Dublin to set up one of the country's top kennels and Paul's lineage surfaces in Newry, Co. Down, where his son Michael McKenna has his kennels.

Ger's father, Malachy, had four sons by his first marriage — Paddy, Joe, Mal and Mike and on the death of his first wife, he married Agnes Gavin. Her people worked for the county council. "They were only ordinary people. Decent old people," says Ger. Malachy's wife gave him nine children, of whom Ger was the first and there followed Marguerite, Frank, Paul, Tim, Mackey, Tony, Philomena and Vincent. Of the first family, Ger was most attached to Mal. On May 6, 1983, Realtin's Best won the Austin Stacks 550 at Tralee. In prestige or prizemoney (IR£4,000), the event did not compare with the £30,000 netted in the English Derby six years later. But trained by Ger McKenna and owned by Mal McKenna, Realtin's Best (Peruvian Style — Realtin) gave the handler one of his most cherished moments in greyhound racing. Mal has since died but for Ger a deep emotional bond still exists. All the McKennas did and continue to keep "a dog or two". But for Ger, it was something different — since that day in 1938, at the age of eight, when he first set foot on a dog track.

Limerick in the south-west is in the heart of doggy country. At the mouth of Ireland's longest river, the Shannon, it lies between County Clare to the north and County Kerry to the south, with counties Cork and Tipperary bordering it inland. Its geographical situation makes it a natural focal point and the city and surrounds provide a readymade catchment area for greyhound racing and coursing.

Ger, aged eight, first accompanied his father Malachy to the track along with a bitch Charity Maid, the daughter of Charity, owned by uncle Joe McKenna in Dublin. The small boy saw over two hundred greyhounds go in six-dog trials, as they all were then. Memory does not recall what Charity Maid clocked. Suffice to say, the youngster was hooked: "From the word go, I never knew nor wanted to know anything else but dogs," said Ger. "I never will know anything else." He does not recall his childhood as being especially happy. "It was tough. After all, there were fifteen of us, all under the same roof," he says, casting his eyes around the house in The Square, which has since been expanded and is now the home of his second son, also Ger, his wife Jennifer and their young son Kevin. The house now incorporates what used to be the house next door. Ger and wife Josie, thirteen years his junior, and the other boys John and Owen have lived for the past ten years in a modern bungalow. Outside, back and front, spruce trees ring immaculately groomed lawns. Ger jokes about watering the plants; Josie interjects that he doesn't do a tap. An IR£27,000 Volvo stands in the drive. The trappings are of comfort rather than of wealth. The atmosphere is convivial. This is a happy house. A home.

Ger went to National School and then Technical School. "I hated it," he says and adds "And I'm not telling a lie" — a characteristic addendum when McKenna wants to emphasise a point. Seamus Gardiner, his National School teacher, would remark: "You only want to be taking a dog by the lead or a calf by the tail." When he was sixteen,

A rare picture of Ger with his father Malachy, his brother Joe and kennelhand Joe Gleeson on the extreme right.

McKenna, the reluctant academic, had left school. After all, Charity Maid had won and McKenna netted twenty-six shillings (£1.30).

"I thought I was a millionaire," he says. "In those days a dog for which you got a couple of hundred pounds was reckoned to be a good dog. They were fed well, but they didn't get prime beef or anything. It was more like sheeps' heads, skimmed milk, potatoes, scraps, brown bread, wheatmeal."

With his father being involved in cattle, McKenna found an easy source of milk. And, as he recounts it, it was much like the cattle business: fatten them up and sell them. The McKennas got the greyhounds ready and sold them off. What Ger learnt from his father was basic and has stood him in good stead.

"I am still doing much the same thing," he says. "The priorities are the same: cleanliness and happiness; and feeding them with the best food you can afford, while always varying their diet."

There is a door in The Square, an ordinary looking brown door, and that leads you through the house and leads you to another square. This is headquarters for arguably the greatest greyhound trainer in the world and, in Irish terms, certainly the most decorated. GHQ.

"Cleanliness and happiness . . . " The words ring in the ear as you take in the white-washed walls and the glossy, black paint on the woodwork. The place is so clean. How could you fail but to be happy here. Perhaps the three McKenna lads — *his army* — do not see it this way. It could be just a job. But there is some greater force at work here, a tradition, a forefather who set the rules. Skirting the courtyard are the houses, each with its purpose, each with food or some tool of the trade. Then you come to a bridge, functional yet delicate. Ger rests his frame against the side of the bridge and looks down at the river, the course of which bisects his kennel complex. At the far side there is the area designated for bitches and another for dogs recovering from injury.

"You haven't done that job as well as the last time," he shouts. Young Ger and Owen are shirtless, knee-high in the flood. They thought their task was over, but now they must wade back into the river, removing the rocks and banking them up at the side.

"Don't want to give the rats places where they can nest," the overseer says by way of explanation of the job in hand.

"So you like working for your father, Owen?" I asked.

"Well, nobody else will work for him, so I suppose . . ."

The old man is not going to be bested: "What he means is that nobody else will have him!"

If you look at Owen McKenna, chubby and baby-faced and not resembling anything like his nineteen years, it is easier to imagine the father, then just turned twenty-two, when he left Borrisokane. It was to be an unlikely alliance between the shy country youth and the big city bookmaker. There is nobody in Ireland who does not know Terry Rogers. He wears loud clothes and when he opens his mouth he is louder still. Rogers grafted his way to the top until his domination of the bookmaking scene in Ireland was total. A newspaper feature on betting in any form, a television debate on any aspect of racing would carry no weight without Rogers having his say. Domestically, Rogers is a legend and, like McKenna, his reputation and influence have spread beyond the Irish shores. These days, Rogers stands less regularly at horse-race meetings and the management of his betting shops has, effectively, been passed to a younger generation. His only involvement in greyhound sport is to be the most colourful layer at the National Coursing Meeting at Clonmel. Rogers' preoccupation is card playing. He runs a qualifier, a trial stake, at home for the World Poker Championships held in Binion's Horseshoe Casino in downtown Las Vegas. For three weeks in early summer it becomes the centrepoint for the globe's high rollers. The man who puts it on is octogenarian Benny Binion, a classic Old West type character. Rogers hugely admires Binion; and the feeling is mutual. But beneath it all, Benny Binion's soul brother is a softy. His bark is truly worse than his bite. It was such a man who saw in Ger McKenna the potential of greatness: "I considered myself a good judge of dogs and people. Ger McKenna did not disappoint me," he says.

In the early Fifties, Rogers was making a book and sidelining as agent for Bill Cutler, a bookmaker and, as Rogers puts it: "He was the nearest thing to a compulsive gambler I have ever come across." Descriptions of Cutler suggest that he, too, was a larger-than-life figure. But Rogers insists: "I had a steadying influence on him. That said, he was the only person I have ever called 'sir' ". The two later went into partnership in a chain of offices in Britain. Cutler at this point had his dogs with Howard Mills near Wolverhampton. Mills was pushing on and Rogers suggested McKenna as a replacement private trainer. McKenna was put in under Mills with the specific task of training Cutler's dogs.

McKenna explains: "I was the kennelman. But, in fact, I was doing it all. Anyway, there was no motorway in those days and you would have to leave at 11.30 am to get to White City by 5.30 pm."

McKenna moved down to Paddy McEvoy who was to win the 1953 English Derby with Daw's Dancer and who was contracted to the Greyhound Racing Association. He took Marsh Harrier, the best of the dogs which Rogers had secured for Cutler. Marsh Harrier was to be both the making and breaking of the young, rookie trainer. Marsh Harrier had beaten the bitch Town Belle by seven lengths. Now at London's Stamford Bridge, a week later, he started at 2-7 favourite to confirm the form. McKenna exonerates Town Belle's trainer Tom Chamberlain of all blame for what happened. The bitch won, with

A young Ger with Marsh Harrier after the dog's win in the 1952 Pall Mall at Harringay with Mrs Billy Cutler (centre) receiving the trophy.

Marsh Harrier and some of the many trophies he won.

Marsh Harrier trailing in twenty-two and a half lengths behind; last in the four-runner race.

"I should have known something was wrong with all my dogs that morning, I should have realised that something was amiss," says McKenna.

The drug test on Marsh Harrier proved positive. Rogers insists that the young McKenna could have stayed on. But the trainer felt he was a marked man with some of the establishment. "I felt uncomfortable. They gave me the push and I came home," he said.

McKenna's contention that he was "too straight and honest," is echoed by Rogers: "Ger was green. I believe he was followed back to the kennels. Once they knew from which kennels he was operating, they could do the business. In fact, to make sure they probably doped all his dogs, all his black dogs anyway. There were a couple of Irish guys involved. Young Ger would probably have been quite happy to talk to somebody from home and perhaps tell him more than he should."

McKenna was on his way back to Borrisokane. A lesson learned. It would never happen again.

Back in Borrisokane, he applied for and was granted his own licence. It was 1956. He recalls the veterinary surgeon Jack Powell calling at the house.

"It was a Monday evening and Jack was talking about a dog owned by Ned Buckley from Nenagh. The price was £150, and I think Jack had it in mind that he and my father would take the dog between them."

Powell was due to come back. But he never returned. He walked out of The Square, bumped into another owner and bought a different dog altogether. In the wonderful and wondrous way that such things happen, McKenna came across Buckley later and negotiated to train the dog which Powell had originally mentioned. McKenna had acquired Prince of Bermuda.

CHAPTER TWO

Family Rivalry

WHETHER through invention or fact, greyhound racing is a jealous game. Where jealousy does not exist there are those only too ready to make it up. The word was, that friendly rivalry between McKenna cousins, Ger in Borrisokane and Gay in Dublin, had developed into something more serious. Gay McKenna was born in 1924, and was Ger's senior by six years. By 1933, the family had moved to Dublin and, in 1942, Gay's father Joe died as a result of a car accident. Gay went to work for his uncle Paul, an established trainer, and then moved to Cabinteely, Co. Dublin. Here, his kennel grew to be the best in the country. The gossip that spread stories of rivalry between the cousins was not peculiar to Irish greyhound circles. The story gathered with the telling. The divide widened.

Gay says: "Of course, there was rivalry. But it never went beyond that. I beat Ger in one Derby final — he beat me in another. I didn't like being beaten — show me the man who does." Ger thinks similarly: "Gay is a very nice man — and was a very good trainer." Before he went to England as private trainer to Bill Cutler, Ger worked for Gay McKenna in Dublin. More than three decades later, Ger McKenna finally succumbed to the agonising pain in his hips and had the hip replacement operation which he had put off for some time. I visited Ger one evening and passed Gay in the hallway. On leaving I assured Ger that I would try and get back to see him again. He replied: "If you can't make it, don't worry. Gay comes in every night before he goes to the dogs." Three decades had spanned their working together. In between they were the best of rivals.

There is a pub in Blanchardstown, called The Greyhound Bar.

Blanchardstown is no longer County Dublin; it is Dublin 15. Part of the great metropolis. A satellite town. Thirty years ago it was rural. Now it has its shopping centre and housing estates; and most of its teenage population has never seen a greyhound. Every morning a tall, distinguished-looking, and well-dressed man will be seen leaving a neat bungalow with a well-tended garden in the main street.

To look at him, you would never think that he was born before greyhound racing. Before the Irish Coursing Club. Before the Republic was christened. But he could tell you the name of the greyhound in the picture displayed in The Greyhound Bar. He was its master. Tom Lynch trained where the shopping centre and The Greyhound Bar now stand, and he took McKenna family rivalry to a new plane.

Tom married Peg McKenna, Gay's sister, in 1946. They met while Tom worked for her father Joe at his Templeogue kennels. In 1953, Tom Lynch acquired the kind of dog which is the stuff of dreams. Spanish Battleship (Spanish Chestnut — Ballyseedy Memory) was sent up from Killorglin in his native Co. Kerry by Tim "Chubb" O'Connor. The Irish Derby in those years was run alternately at Harold's Cross and Shelbourne Park and in 1953 it was the turn of Cross. In the final, Spanish Battleship, as was his style, made all the running in 29.78. At Shelbourne Park, the next year, Spanish Battleship improved his clock even further when triumphing in 29.64. Back to Harold's Cross again and the hat-trick attempt. Even more remarkable than his actual winning was that he was faster still, in 29.53. The only dog in the decider to match his early pace was kennel companion Dancing Jester. In seventy-five starts, Spanish Battleship was first sixty-one times.

It took Tom Lynch twelve years to find another Derby winner. But Russian Gun (Pigalle Wonder — Shandaroba) gave him his fourth Blue Riband in 1967 in a time of 29.44 at Harold's Cross. It took the record 29.11 of Yellow Printer at Shelbourne Park to relegate Russian Gun to second spot in the following year — and Johnny Bassett had based Yellow Printer with Gay McKenna! Tom's Down Signal had run up controversially to Clonbonny Bridge in 30.53 at Shelbourne Park in 1944. These were pre-photo-finish days and many felt that the judge could have awarded the decision to the Lynch dog. Dead-heats were unheard of then. In 1946, at Shelbourne Park, Lynch's Bohernagraga Boy ran in the final won in 30.20 by Steve. Then in 1951 came the extraordinary feat of getting three through to the decider — Dooneen

The McKenna Classic Tree

55 classics from 1935 to 1989

Malachy
(b. 1888 d. 1964)

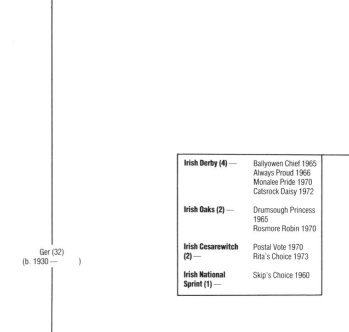

Irish Derby (4) —	Ballyowen Chief 1965
	Always Proud 1966
	Monalee Pride 1970
	Catsrock Daisy 1972
Irish Oaks (2) —	Drumsough Princess 1965
	Rosmore Robin 1970
Irish Cesarewitch (2) —	Postal Vote 1970
	Rita's Choice 1973
Irish National Sprint (1) —	Skip's Choice 1960

Ger (32)
(b. 1930 —   )

English Derby (2) —	Parkdown Jet 1981	Produce	Big Kuda 1973
	Lartigue Note 1989	Stakes (2) —	Cill Dubh Darkey 1976
Irish Derby (3) —	Own Pride 1969	Irish	Butterfly Billy 1965
	Bashful Man 1973	Cesarewitch (4) —	Yanka Boy 1967
	Rathgallen Tady 1987		Ballybeg Prim 1975
			Oughter Brigg 1987
Irish Oaks (1) —	Nameless Pixie 1979		
		Irish National	Bauhus 1965
Irish St Leger (12) —	Prince of Bermuda 1956	Sprint (2) —	Move Gas 1969
	Swanlands Best 1960		
	Apollo Again 1962	Irish Laurels (6) —	Gabriel Boy 1970
	Lovely Chieftain 1965		Nameless Star 1976
	Yanka Boy 1967		Knockrour Slave 1980
	Own Pride 1969		Back Garden 1983
	Time Up Please (2) 1971,		Rugged Mick 1984
	'72		Follow A Star 1985
	Ballybeg Prim 1975		
	Nameless Star 1976		
	Red Rasper 1977		
	Moran's Beef 1984		

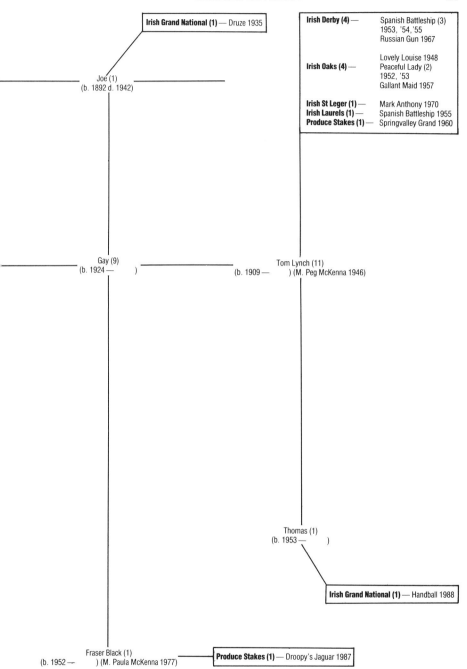

This is no ordinary dog

Money cannot buy him!

THE telephone in the home (Killorglin 14) of Mr. Timothy ("Chub") O'Connor (picture inset above) was ringing urgently. When Mr. O'Connor answered it he was told to hold on for a call from London. "This is Major Baker speaking," said a voice, "and I am acting on behalf of a syndicate hoping to buy Spanish Battleship."

*The great Spanish Battleship, winner of three Irish Derbies,
trained by Tom Lynch.*

Miss, Noble Greason, and Locht Seal. The last named topped the trio in second but this Harold's Cross final went to Carmody's Tanist in 29.64. Tom's Monalee Gambler chased home Ger's Own Pride — 29.20 at Harold's Cross — in 1969 while Menelaus took a supporting role as, in 1970 at Shelbourne Park, Gay's Monalee Pride and Ger's Own Pride contested the finish in 29.28. The Blanchardstown man's Kal's Daisy finished behind Ger's Bashful Man, the 28.82 winner in 1973. Tom Lynch was certainly not the type of man to begrudge that Gay McKenna would win as many Derby trophies. Nor that Ger McKenna would soon set off in pursuit of the record.

"Tom Lynch is a true sportsman and a true gentleman," says Ger.

In 1932 Gay McKenna attended his first Irish Greyhound Derby final. His first and *the* first. Guidless Joe won at Shelbourne Park in

*Ballyowen Chief; winner of the 1965 Irish Derby. Pat Dalton receives the
Greyhound of the Year Trophy, trainer Gay, is holding the dog.*

Ringsend in 30.36 and, for the record, was owned by Jack Moylan who was placed on Fly Mask in the 1925 Aintree Grand National and who rode a winner of every Irish Flat classic. Like the McKennas, Jack Moylan was a link in a great racing tradition and Pat Eddery is his grandson. Gay's father Joe had sent Buzzing Dick out to run up the Irish Derby to 30.45 winner Frisco Hobo in 1934, with kennel companion Seldom At Home also in the race. Joe had finalists in Guidless Joe's first Derby and an also-ran to Shelbourne Park 30.52 scorer Monalogue in the following year.

Gay says: "For the life of me, I cannot recall the names of my father's runners in the first two years of the Derby at Shelbourne Park. I know I was a very small boy and that uncle Paul, who was a fine big man, used to lift me up to see the dogs on the track. Of course, the family lived mostly in Birr in the early years. The racing season was very short in those days — just six months — and my father used to stay in Templeogue and come back down during the winter. I can recall the point at which my father Joe started to concentrate on the dogs more. He was dealing in cattle when there was an outbreak of Foot and Mouth disease. If your cattle were contaminated, you got compensation. If not, they simply went into quarantine. Ours were not infected, and were subsequently worth little or nothing when they came out of quarantine. It was a very bad blow."

Gay's sister Peg remembers the year that her father Joe won his only classic, the Irish Grand National with Druze. "I remember that we were all very anxious to see the cup being presented. But we were whisked off home because it was so late. The next morning we were given plenty of lemonade. When the family was in Templeogue, we went down to see uncle Malachy in Borrisokane. It was a great occasion then. It took three and a half hours to get to Borrisokane and the long journey added to the excitement." Peg recalls being conscious of the fact that uncle Malachy had married again: "But it was as if the children did not realise it. The two families played so happily together."

It was in 1961 at Harold's Cross that Gay's Skip's Choice went closer still to following Guidless Joe into the annals when caught near the line by Chieftain's Guest in 29.45. In 1964, his runner Gleaming There was a beaten finalist at Shelbourne Park when Wonder Valley clocked 29.30. Ballyowen Chief (Oregon Prince — Earnest Lady) was the first Derby winner to be trained by a McKenna when successful in 29.42 at

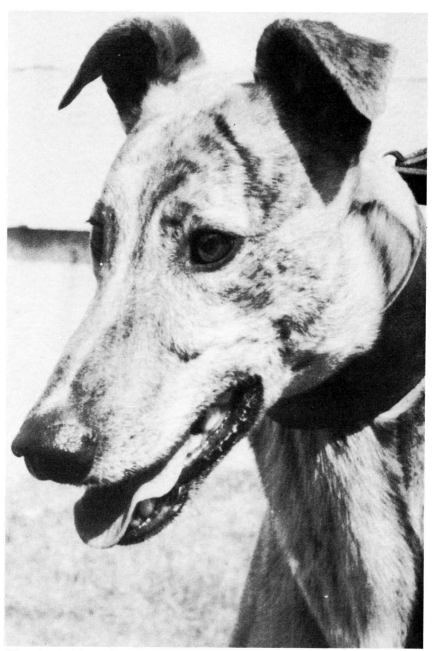

Monalee Pride: Winner of the 1970 Irish Derby, trained by Gay McKenna.

Paula McKenna with Postal Vote, runner-up in the 1971 Irish Derby, trained by her father Gay.

Harold's Cross in 1965. The following year, at Shelbourne Park, Gay went even better when Always Proud (Clonalvy Pride — Always A Rebel) beat his other runner Tiger Chief in 29.44. In the strange way that the McKenna cousins' lives have always seemed to criss-cross, it was Gay's winner Always Proud which sired Ger's first successful finalist Own Pride (Always Proud — Kitty True), the 29.20 winner at Harold's Cross in 1969; Gay had Finola's Yarn and Kilbelin Grand here. Twelve months later, Own Pride was relegated to second by Gay's Monalee Pride (Prairie Flash — Sheila Atlast) in 29.28, in the year that the Irish Derby found its permanent home at Shelbourne Park and its first sponsor, the cigarette makers Carrolls of Dundalk. Gay's Postal Vote was second to Sole Aim in 29.12 at Shelbourne Park in 1971; but the Dublin-based McKenna would not be thwarted next year when the bitch Catsrock Daisy (Fantastic Prince — Truly Silver) won in 29.20. In 1973, it was Ger and Gay head-to-head again. Gay had the great Rita's Choice; but Ger came up with the sensational 28.82 winner Bashful Man (Myross Again — Ballyflake). Black Bart, in 1977, was the last Gay McKenna-trained finalist in an Irish Derby and Linda's Champion won that year in 29.53. Then Ger's city cousin retired and handed over the leads to his own son who, if one was not too confused already, was named Ger McKenna. These days you will find him on the racecard as G.J. McKenna.

Gay McKenna equalled his brother-in-law Tom Lynch's record of four Irish Derby wins. Gay twice won the Irish Oaks (Drumsough Prince in 1965 and Rosmore Robin in 1970) and the Irish Cesarewitch (Postal Vote in 1970 and Rita's Choice in 1973) as well as the Irish National Sprint with Skip's Choice (1960). In the year in which he fielded his last Irish Derby finalist, Fraser Black married Gay's daughter Paula. In 1987, Scottish-born Black, based at Rathangan, Co. Kildare, sent Droopy's Jaguar out to win the National Breeders Two-Year-Old Produce Stakes. Tom Lynch matched his own Derby performance by winning the Irish Oaks four times — Lovely Louisa (1948), Peaceful Lady (1952 and '53) and Gallant Maid (1957). Spanish Battleship also gave him an Irish Laurels in 1955, while success followed in the Irish St. Leger with Mark Anthony (1970) and Produce Stakes with Sprinvalley Grand (1960). Tom and Peg Lynch need not have worried about the classic tradition fading on their branch of the family tree. In 1988, less than two years after he had taken over from his

brother Gerard, who had stepped into his father's shoes before leaving
to work with Dick Andrews in America, Thomas Lynch provided three
runners in the final of the Irish Grand National and won it with
Handball.But when these two great men, Gay McKenna and Tom
Lynch, decided to retire, Ger McKenna's quest for classic winners had
already brought his tally into double figures — and he was chasing hard
to equal the record which they shared — that of turning out four Irish
Derby winners.

CHAPTER THREE

The Trainer

THEY call Ger McKenna names. They say he is cute, always one move ahead — and . . . some of what they say may even be true. Once he was "too straight and honest"; and it landed him back in Borrisokane, a wiser man. He would never be anyone's mug again. McKenna could, if reflecting on his first and unsatisfactory sojourn in England, pinpoint where he went wrong. A word about where Marsh Harrier was kennelled. The giveaway. Perhaps it was this that has made him a less than bubbling conversationalist in the company of strangers.

Pictorial evidence supports the assertion. If McKenna is in the picture, he is in the background; and backing away. Perhaps I am reading too much into it all. But the Marsh Harrier affair must have left its mark. Nowadays, McKenna talks more. Talks, but says little. He tells only what he wants you to know. He is more outgoing, while at the same time feeling uncomfortable in places like the restaurant in Wimbledon on race nights. He would prefer to be down in the crowd. Anonymous. The pre-Derby lunch at Wimbledon is a nightmare. He is the centre of attention, yet he would rather be back with the dogs, who will not let him down, sell him out or use his words for their own gains . . . He is uncomfortable. But he makes the effort. McKenna is well-off and respected. It is a state which leaves him less vulnerable. Money and fame cushion him from the "nobblers". He remains, at the same time, very human. Understanding and understandable. Human, but no saint. Then again, there are not too many who have put a lead on a dog who are saints. Greyhound racing, with attractive prize money and more per capita betting than its equine brother, is not on the approved road to canonisation.

A relaxed Ger.   *Steve Nash*

"My mother was a saint," says McKenna. "The amount of work she went through with fifteen of us, it was tough, you know. There would be a pot over the fire in the kitchen; that was the only heat we had in the house. And if something went wrong, if the pot spilled over, we would have to build the fire back up again. Tough times, I'll tell ye."

After Marsh Harrier, he was back in the family fold and, one suspects, happy and relieved to be so. He was tougher, too, from the years with Gay in Cabinteely and Howard Mills in Wolverhampton. He was coming into his own as a trainer and had his own ideas. His father still held the licence. Prince of Bermuda (1956) and Daring Customer (1958), between the years of Tom Lynch's treble with Spanish Battleship and Gay McKenna's great Irish Derby run, ran up the premier classic as representing the kennel of Malachy McKenna. But it was Ger who was doing the dogs and, while it is a technical point, nobody regards Prince of Bermuda, or any subsequent Borrisokane runner, as anything but trained by Ger McKenna. Perhaps it was the sort of situation which would lead to internal tensions, as it would in any other household; in any other family business. The old man and the young son anxious to get on.

"My father was as keen as anyone that I should get along," says Ger. "There came a point when he wanted me to set up in Dublin. We even had a place picked out in Chapelizod. He felt that Dublin was the place to be, with two big tracks and everything. But I didn't want to go. I could have made England my base. But when things didn't work out there, there was nowhere else apart from Borrisokane that I wanted to be. I decided I would stay in Borrisokane."

Peg Lynch, his first cousin recalls: "There is one picture I remember, one of Ger on O'Connell Bridge in Dublin. He was the image of Owen now, except perhaps smaller." Ger McKenna had seen Dublin. He had his picture taken on O'Connell Bridge — a picture as obligatory as those taken with the Eiffel Tower in Paris or Tower Bridge in London as the backdrop. But he decided he would settle for Borrisokane.

With the benefit of time gone by, Ger volunteers a kind of insight, a reflective glance back at what might have been with his father. It is almost a wistful longing to go back and start the relationship all over again. Only the death of either party ends the tension; and because of what has gone before, the sense of loss, the frustration of not being able to undo what has been done, is profound; heartbreaking.

Ger, John and Owen at work in the McKenna kennel complex. Recipients of the magic McKenna touch are Tomijo, Angelo Carlotti, Heather's Best and Attractive Son.   *Steve Nash*

Studying The Form . . . Ger scans the racing papers.   *Steve Nash*

"My father was a fine man, one of the finest," he says. "Perhaps I did not appreciate him at the time, perhaps I could have been more respectful. I hope both he and my mother are in heaven." Silence . . . Malachy McKenna died in 1964 at the age of seventy-six and yet, twenty-five years on, it is probably the first time that Ger has spoken this way. Aloud. He is a complex man, yet in order to understand his dogs, you must understand the man, for only then can you appreciate how he gets the best from his charges. I recall an early incident in my career when a greyhound fought in an Irish Derby preliminary — it had a go in the holy of holies, Shelbourne Park, and in the Blue Riband, too. Now that was news. Naturally, it was the sort of coverage which the owner of the disgraced animal did not appreciate. He sent a cryptic message saying I could mention his wife in any unfavourable light I chose . . . "only leave my dogs out of it!" Greyhound racing is thus. The relationship between man and dog is total, they become one. To praise the dog is to praise the man — and vice versa. It is totally true of McKenna. His dogs are genuine as the man is himself. They are a mirror image.

Away from the hurly-burly of the city, with non-stop traffic going by your door, Borrisokane is a quiet backwater. You could sleep well here — but not Ger McKenna. Time is money when you are working for yourself. Your own master — and master of three sons who also look to you for a living wage. The days follow a strict routine.

7.00 am: Down to the paddock. Let the dogs out. They will go out at two-hour intervals after that. Ger and the boys have a light breakfast of tea and toast. "We're barred from having a fry-up that early in the morning," says Ger and sort of leaves the sentence hanging, so that you have to ask: Why? "Because there is no way I'm cooking one that early," says his wife Josie. The kennels are swept out.

9.00 am: The dogs' breakfast. A mish-mash. A wonderous concoction blended over the years. Trial and error until you get "a dog's dinner" of a breakfast which includes: white and brown bread, sherry, honey, raw eggs, chicken and cornflakes. There are no popular commercial brands, in quantity anyway. "Maybe a bit of Kasco by way of a change. I am not a great believer in the usual brands. I haven't been since my father's time," says Ger, Master Chef.

The boys can have something more substantial themselves now. "It's a family team. No one else would really fit in," says father . . . "You really need people, the lads, who have a vested interest in the place . . . Your own are your own."

11.00 am: The dogs have been out in the paddock again. It is grooming time — teeth, nails, combing, rubbing.

12.00 pm: Steep the bread now and prepare the main meal of the day and then it's home for lunch. There are no chances taken. Gates are locked and a German Shepherd dog stands guard. "If he weren't with one of us, it would take the leg off you," Ger says with that mischievous grin of his.

1.00 pm: Lunch break.

2.00 pm: Back to the paddocks. There is much to be done. Injured dogs to be cared for: getting them back into shape; giving them some light work. A gallop. McKenna dogs are seldom road-walked. The sprint trial or the gallop is preferred.

3.30 pm: The main meal. Variety is the key. The basics are cooked meat, raw meat, minced beef. Once a week there will be chicken or some other substitute "They are much like yourself. They like a change," says the man who designed the menu: " It will be mixed with soup one day and fresh vegetable the next." Of course, the dogs racing that evening will not dine: "Just a pinch. A drop of tea just to keep the hunger off them."

4.00 pm: Shower and change and get ready to go to Dublin, Cork . . . wherever. It is one hundred miles to Dublin one way, the same to Cork in the other direction . . ." "You're not near anywhere, but you're central," says Ger.

9.00 pm: Whoever does not go racing stays behind to keep an eye on things and lets the dogs out for the last time before nightfall. By and large, they will not wet their bedding at night but Ger prefers if they relieve themselves. "Most are house-trained, but their kidneys will suffer." The bedding is shredded computer paper. The motto: "Keep them happy; keep them clean".

12.30 am: Arrive home from racing and bed.

Apart from race experience, the best test for a greyhound is a gallop. In complete privacy, a trainer can put a dog through its paces, assess its potential and decide on its future course. McKenna is a passionate believer in galloping greyhounds and he has a special place where he takes them. It is a rare privilege for anyone outside the immediate McKenna circle to witness the dogs at work. McKenna knows the route well and unhesitatingly negotiates the tight corners and narrow streets of sleepy hamlets as he cuts the path to his destination, zig-zagging as if trying to elude a pursuer. The van is driven by son Ger with Owen and grandson Kevin as passengers. A sharp and unexpected turn left and down the boreen. Bog is an oft misused word. Frequently linked to the Irish in a derisory way, it seldom, in local terms, refers to marshy or watery ground. It is quite simply a bog or large tract of flat land from which turf is cut. There is a sameness about every yard of this treeless plain. But we head for one spot; a spot tried and trusted. We get out and look around; and you could be standing five months earlier at Altcar, on a vastness that they call The Withins. But instead of grass, your feet are on the brown earth which next year will be burning in the hearths of Ireland. An all-weather gallop; a bog which, ironically, would be useless to the trainer when winter's rainfall softens it so much that the greyhound's feet go too deeply into the pile. This is The Bog, to which McKenna will continually refer. This is his place, his preserve, where he will happily gallop his priceless canines, all the game's household names, when to take them to race or trial at the schooling track would constitute too great a risk. This time he has four dogs in all — a pup about which the trainer, as yet, knows little; the potentially brilliant Tomijo and Annacurra Hill; and the experienced Radio Sport (which was formerly Dandy Duke before transferring to the names of Pat O'Donovan, Miceal O'Muircheartaigh, Michael Fortune and Ruth Buchanan of the RTE Radio greyhound broadcasts team).

The routine is well known. The gallop lies between two drains and Owen goes off in front, the scout, looking for the stone which might cause catastrophe and the piece of paper which might distract the dog in its trial. Owen has gone up over three hundred yards. His more athletic brother Ger waits and then goes in pursuit, sprinting, the whistle in his mouth, tooting its shrill sound between breaths. With his right hand he frantically waves a rabbit skin, like a Red Indian in a ritual dance. The dogs are crazed, coltishly bucking up and down, straining on their leads. McKenna releases one to the care of Tom Dooley. Tom is the porter in the Allied Irish Bank in Borrisokane, a job which demands a high degree of confidentiality. A job to which Tom is well suited. Tom is friendly, yet silent. He has been a McKenna associate for quarter of a century. He will give nothing away. He takes the pup in strong hands, ties the lead in make-shift coursing slips. "Let him go now, Tom," says the boss; and off he goes. He trundles at pull pace towards the sound of the whistle and the sight of the skin and pulls up abruptly. Tomijo and Radio Sport, too.

Annacurra Hill (I'm Slippy — Dusty Fever) was bought with Eddie Costello in mind but he has been plagued by injury since winning in 29.36 over 525 yards at Shelbourne Park. McKenna had decided to try and confine his runs to the all-sanded Clonmel in the hope of keeping him sound. But he again shows lameness after a sprint at the Co. Tipperary venue. McKenna has been typically patient and not raced him since early May. He decides to pull him out on this Thursday evening in mid-July. The white and black strains at the leash — and away. Suddenly, a hand shoots up involuntarily, as it would in the last minutes before an unavoidable head-on collision between two vehicles. Annacurra Hill is listing, his right legs desperately trying to grip the ground to keep him upright. He cannot prevent a further lunge to the right and just corrects himself in time, so as to avoid toppling into the drain. The dog lobs along to where the boys are and takes no stopping. McKenna shakes his head. For the most part he is pensive on the way back in the car. In anticipation of better things, Annacurra Hill had been entered for the Golden Vale 360, an open sprint, at Shelbourne Park on the following Monday. McKenna confined himself to: "Well, he's trying his best," to those who enquired as to the dog's chances. It was not taken to be a vote of confidence.

The betting centred around the dog from trap one which had scored in 19.52 for the trip, a decent run; and there was money for trap six. Annacurra Hill, running from trap five, was friendless and allowed to drift out to 5-2. There is a point at which logic clouds and merges into the inexplicable. There is a point where a trainer will cease to be able to actually say why a dog will win for him. He just has it; whatever that great indefinable "it" is. In the greater order of things, the Golden Vale 360 was an insignificant race and Annacurra Hill an also-ran in the catalogue of McKenna's canine immortals. Suffice to say that, four days after his shoulder gave way and he hovered precariously at the edge of the drain, Annacurra Hill won the Golden Vale 360 by a short head from the favourite.

CHAPTER FOUR

Prince of Bermuda

PRINCE of Bermuda is the key greyhound in the career of Ger McKenna. He is the link between ambition and its realisation. At the same time, he is something more profound. The year 1955 was the dawning of a new era in a sport under semi-State control. A post-war society was emerging from the shadow of Church domination, like children throwing off the yoke of parental discipline. There was more money about and the good times were about to roll for a young population; greyhound racing; and Ger McKenna. It was as if the arrival of Prince of Bermuda on the scene was fated. Although in fact, the dog was not welcomed with open arms. Ger, who had applied for his own licence by then, remembers debating with his father as to whether they had room for another greyhound; and one which did not immediately strike them as above average. Ger eventually agreed to take Prince of Bermuda from Ned Buckley. On the day he arrived, the dog had run seven races and on his last outing he had been unplaced in 31.50 for 525 yards. McKenna must have had some sort of inkling about the dog's potential. He was keen enough to give him a trial on a Good Friday — something which was completely taboo.

"We had another very useful dog here at the time, Crafty Killer owned by Martin Divilly. Prince of Bermuda ran away from him," recalls Ger who has another good reason to remember the trial.

"It was expressly forbidden by my father to try dogs on Sunday or any holy day. He ate me that day," says Ger, adding that his father was still not adverse to clouting the boys even if they were in their twenties.

It was the opening of an unofficial and unrecognised track at Chapelizod on the outskirts of Dublin that broke the Sunday embargo.

Ger with Ned Buckley and the great Prince of Bermuda, the trainer's first classic winner.

Sunday night was the big night at the flapping track and no matter what
the big wigs in Shelbourne Park said about it, or what they
threatened, the place thrived. "Every decent dog in the country was
raced there," says Ger. Sunday racing was, ironically, to be expressly
precluded when, three years later, Bord na gCon came into being,
armed with the Greyhound Industry Act (1958). But for a few, short,
eventful seasons, Chapelizod was the focal point for greyhound
followers on Sunday nights. Ger McKenna soon set off for Chapelizod
with Prince of Bermuda, who won easily. "The time was 29.60 or
something close to that. A great run for Chapelizod." A few nights later,
Prince of Bermuda went "legit" and was entered for a race at
Shelbourne Park. Paddy O'Donoghue, then the all-powerful manager
of the Ringsend Stadium, mentioned to Ger that he had heard the dog
had run well at Chapelizod. "I just gave him the deaf one," says Ger.
The race was won in 29.80 and the price was 3-1. Prince of Bermuda
had definitely arrived. "We knew now that he was the best dog we had
had. He won the Kennedy Cup, which was over 550 yards at Limerick
then, and also the McAlinden Cup, which was over 525 yards at
Shelbourne Park." Prince of Bermuda wintered well, and when he
made his seasonal reappearance for 1956 he had lost none of his zip. His
first race, a sprint over 360 yards at Shelbourne Park, was taken in
20.10. "That was a great run at the time," says Ger. The Irish St Leger
preceded the other major classics in those days and Prince of Bermuda
(Champion Prince — Sunora) was Ger McKenna's first classic winner
and first winner of the 550 yards Limerick feature, which he has
dominated since. When Moran's Beef triumphed in 1984, McKenna
had won the Irish St Leger on a dozen occasions. Nothing like Prince of
Bermuda's time of 30.66 had ever been recorded in the final of the Irish
St Leger and it would take another McKenna charge, Time Up
Please, to better the clock in the Limerick classic, recording 30.56, and
that was not until 1971.

The British were before their time in introducing metrication to track
distances and the Irish were in no great hurry to follow. The reason was
simple: The standard distance was 525 yards. The standard time was
thirty seconds. It was quite straightforward. If your greyhound ran
outside thirty seconds, he was average; if he ran inside thirty seconds,
he was above average. It was something to which everyone could relate.
It is thus easy to appreciate the mirth caused by Des Hanrahan, soon to

be Bord na gCon chairman, when, as a journalist with the provincial *Limerick Leader*, he suggested that Prince of Bermuda was capable of breaking twenty-nine seconds at Shelbourne Park.

"Des had written to the effect that if ever a dog was going to beat twenty-nine seconds at Ringsend, then Prince of Bermuda would be the one to do it. Everybody laughed," says Ger, who laughed louder still when the dog actually did it. "It was big news at the time. I remember one of the papers carrying a cartoon of Paddy O'Donoghue, looking at his watch in amazement."

It was a short and congested season. The Irish Derby followed immediately after the Irish St Leger, in July. Even now, one can appreciate the enormity of Prince of Bermuda's feat. Just two years earlier Spanish Battleship had established a new Shelbourne Park mark at 29.50. On July 21, 1956, Keep Moving — which was vying with Prince of Bermuda for the honour of being regarded as the fastest greyhound in training — notched a new track record in 29.40. The Irish Derby was underway. The next heat was won in 29.76, and then Prince of Bermuda went into action. He ran away with the preliminary and as contemporary reports relate, there was a slight delay in announcing the time, for Paddy O'Donoghue was looking at his clock in amazement! *The Sporting Press* reported that the crowd was alive to the possibility that the record had gone again. The figures, two and eight, went up to an ecstatic reception: 28.98. In the semi-finals, a packed Shelbourne Park was treated to the duel which they wanted — between Prince of Bermuda and Keep Moving. They made Prince of Bermuda favourite and he was a decisive winner. But the August 11 decider was to see that result reversed. Prince of Bermuda, in trap six could not repeat his flying start of a week before. Keep Moving in one, just held the vital first bend lead and practically won by the same distance by which he had been beaten at the penultimate stage. McKenna was bitterly disappointed: "We were young at that time and less well able to take it," he says.

Keep Moving went on to win the classic Irish National Sprint at Dunmore Stadium in Belfast before being retired to stud with ironically, Malachy McKenna in Borrisokane. But Prince of Bermuda would race on in record-breaking style. In 1956, the Irish Laurels was, as always, run at Cork; but the distance was 500 yards and would be until 1961 when it changed over to the now conventional 525 yards. In an Irish Laurels heat, Prince of Bermuda became the only greyhound ever to break twenty-eight seconds for the Cork classic trip when winning in 27.95. They no longer run over 500 yards at Cork and it is a record which still stands. But the same fate was to befall the first of the McKenna champions that he had experienced in the Irish Derby. In the final of the Irish Laurels, Prince of Bermuda ran up to Rather Grand.

Yet, Prince of Bermuda still had a significant role to play in the development of his young trainer. Ned Buckley, the farmer cum insurance broker who had persuaded a not-too-enthusiastic McKenna to take the dog, was to re-direct his life again. Buckley accepted an invitation to an International Challenge at White City. Ger McKenna, who had quit Britain disillusioned three years earlier, was going back. Already, the London crowd had taken him to their hearts. "We got a great reception, both before and after the race," Ger recalls. The trio for the challenge were all by Champion Prince. Opposing Prince of Bermuda were: Defence Leader, sent out by Tom Reilly (Walthamstow), and Northern King, trained by Jack Harvey (Wembley). Over the 525 yards of hallowed turf, Prince of Bermuda made every yard of the running. Ger McKenna had arrived . . . Ger McKenna was back.

McKenna will often say in his off-hand, modest way that "anyone can train a good greyhound." It is a phrase which could contain some germ of truth; but many good greyhounds have failed to give their best until put into the correct hands. Prince of Bermuda is a glaring example of this. But there is the other side, which sets the trainer apart from his fellows. It is the ability to take the average greyhound and make him into a champion. Sometimes a sportsman is pushed into a corner, and the only thing that will secure his release is saying what his interrogator, who quite often comes in the shape of a journalist, wants to hear. How many times have we seen a jockey, out of breath, collared on the subject of the exact ability of the horse he has just ridden to victory in the Epsom Derby? For many it is a once-in-a-lifetime moment, one which they cannot fully savour. The head is muddled and a thousand thoughts race through. How did Roberto compare to Nijinsky, Golden Fleece to Grundy, Nashwan to Henbit? In some ways it is a stupid question. The shrewd jockey will be thinking about his percentages, about flattering the owner of the winner; about future rides; about the massive stud fees that will follow. You are not going to know the truth. You will not fare

Ger pictured with Swanlands Best at White City in 1960 with John O'Dwyer and John Delahunty.

much better with the novice rider. He is not in a position to compare like with like; and, anyway, he is too excited to think straight. Ger McKenna has often been asked to draw such comparisons. He has probably been quizzed on this very point after leading in every one of his thirty-one classics winners after Prince of Bermuda. Is he better? Is he the best? Given a span of over thirty years, differences in age, style of running, distance, going, track and all the other variables, it is preposterous to ask the definitive question and expect the definitive answer. Tell us, Ger, what was the *best* greyhound you ever trained? For the most part he will choose to be diplomatic, not to offend the owner (even if he is no longer a patron) and not to offend the memory of a greyhound which may not have been great but had his good points, nevertheless. In between: "that fella was a right bastard of a dog" and "he was one of the best I ever trained", there are those which just won.

Swanlands Best (Man of Pleasure — Swanland's Neighbour) gave McKenna his second Irish St Leger winner in 1960. He was owned by Thurles publican Jack Dwyer and John Delahunty, who was a director of Thurles dog track. Thurles held occasional sales at that time and Swanlands Best was purchased there for £60. When he went to White City for the Anglo-Irish International, the owners were offered £12,000, but turned it down. McKenna recalls that the dog had an exceptionally bad card. He later concluded that the dog was none too genuine either. Perhaps anyone could have trained Prince of Bermuda. But McKenna got Swanlands Best to win the Irish St Leger in 31.60 — almost a full second slower than the time achieved by Prince of Bermuda four years earlier. Two years later Apollo Again (Knockrour Again — Rendondo Beach) was even less memorable.

"I think he was owned by people called Grace in Pallasgrean, Co. Limerick," says Ger. "I don't remember a great deal about him. He was a great-looking dog, but surly with it. The Leger was nearly the first event we ran him in. I do remember we had a bitch in the same final. She got hurt and we had to withdraw her."

The year was 1962 and the classic was won in 31.26. Well, let us not be too hard on old Apollo Again. He did, after all, pay for a honeymoon. The thirty-two-year-old trainer married Josephine Loughnane, thirteen years his junior, from Birr, Co. Offaly, who had opened up a hairdressing salon in Borrisokane.

Lovely Chieftain (Knockhill Chieftain — Lovely Sister), St Leger

"The day I lost my independence," as Josie puts it. The new Mrs McKenna helps to cut the cake after her wedding on the Fourth of July, 1962.

winner in 1965 remains a more kind memory. The dog was owned by Pat Dalton, Golden, Co. Tipperary, who had gone, at the behest of Bord na gCon, to set up kennels in America in 1961. Dalton was to be Ireland's roving ambassador, bringing out dogs, winning with them and thus advertising the breed. It was a sound move by the then Board. It was a good deal, all round. The costs were proportionately high, but the rewards in the USA were staggering. Dalton became a wealthy man and Bord na gCon had its passport into the North American market. Meanwhile, at home — on his own doorstep more or less — Dalton had the uniquely talented top trainer McKenna handling his greyhounds. Ger went to Limerick to meet Dalton, who was handing over his Lovely Arrow to the man from Borrisokane. Lovely Arrow's brother Lovely Chieftain was running in a heat of the Irish St Leger on the night. He qualified but ran poorly and Dalton asked his fellow Tipperaryman to take the dog home, too. So, Lovely Chieftain is unusual in that he was already in the St Leger, in Dalton's care, before McKenna set eyes on him. This is the only time that McKenna recalls this happening in a classic, although it was in similar circumstances that he acquired Yanka Boy during the Midland Puppy Stakes in Mullingar. Lovely Chieftain won the St Leger in 30.92, and was a cut above Swanlands Best and Apollo Again. McKenna believes he was of the same calibre as Prince of Bermuda, but just days after his Limerick success, Lovely Chieftain broke his leg contesting the Irish Derby at Harold's Cross. The smash occurred off the rails at the third bend.

"He looked all over a winner, but he would never come back," says Ger. "The leg was in smithereens."

McKenna has always had an eye for a dog even when its record is not that spectacular. This was the case with Yanka Boy (Clonalvy Pride — Millie Hawthorn) the St Leger winner in 1967. Ger saw him race on a Saturday night at Shelbourne Park where he recorded at mediocre time of 30.42.

"He just took my fancy," says Ger. "We went off to Mullingar on the following Tuesday and bought him for £600 out of the first round of the Midland Puppy Stake. He turned out to be a good winner of the Irish St Leger. Along with Rathgallen Tady, he was probably the widest runner I ever trained. But Limerick wasn't that wide so he was kept in." His winning time was 30.77.

McKenna believes it was Yanka Boy's wide running that cost him the

Josie with Ballykilty. The dog held the track record at 28.80 for 525 yards at Shelbourne Park.

Ger and Josie with sons Ger and John after the 1967 Irish Cesarewitch success of Yanka Boy.

Derby, in the same year. But he made up for it by becoming the trainer's first dual classic winner when he went to Navan to claim the Irish Cesarewitch.

"It was a very congested calendar in those days. But you had to have a go or leave them at home," McKenna remarks.

After Navan, Yanka Boy was sold to Mattie Costello at Borrisoleigh, Co. Tipperary, and was put to stud. The McKennas had Always Proud and Proud Lincoln standing at stud and their owner, Albert Lucas, had asked that they would take no other stud dogs. Ger honoured that request. "But I was always sorry that I did not keep Yanka Boy," he says.

Good trainers attract good dogs, and what is equally important, they attract good owners. At about this time McKenna was gathering excellent connections, the type that could afford to buy top dogs, keep them in training, and who were genuinely enthusiastic about the sport. Mick Loughnane, the Roscrea, Co. Tipperary butcher, the owner of Yanka Boy falls into this category. He had the distinction of owning not only the kennel's first dual classic winner, but also the only McKenna greyhound to win the same classic in successive years. The greyhound was Time Up Please (Newdown Heather — Dogstown Fame) who was bought at the Shelbourne Park Sales for £700, a fair deal of money at the time. His St Leger preparation consisted of the now almost obligatory drive to the Midland Puppy Stake in Mullingar, and a couple of runs in Shelbourne Park. A familiar build-up was now in place. Mullingar–Shelbourne Park–Limerick. The Dublin outings proved particularly revealing. Time Up Please was entered in a twelve-dog stake and won his eliminator in 29.04. On the same night, Ballykilty — a greyhound for which McKenna has retained a great admiration — clocked 29.25. Time Up Please took the final in 29.08. In that sort of form he reached the Irish Derby final and won the Irish St Leger in 30.56. It was 1971 and the best return in an Irish St Leger decider since Prince of Bermuda in 1956. He could only manage 31.05 when he held on to his St Leger crown the following year, but he more than made up the time deficit when he won the new feature, the International 525 in Dundalk, in 29.60. Even by today's standards it was an excellent run. But Time Up Please was not the easiest of dogs to train.

"He was a hard dog to get right; and a hard dog to keep right," says McKenna.

The 1971 Irish St Leger Trophy is presented to Josie McKenna, minutes after Mick Loughnane, the owner of Time Up Please, had collapsed and died.

Ballybeg Prim, winner of the Irish St Leger, Irish Cesarewitch, and Guinness 600 and Irish Greyhound of the Year in 1975, and Tantallon's Flyer, winner of the Easter Cup in the same year.   *Ruth Rogers*

Tragically, owner Mick Loughnane's enthusiasm for the sport took the ultimate toll. As Time Up Please crossed the line at Limerick's Market's Field, the owner came over to McKenna to congratulate him. "He hardly had the words out, when he fell into my arms and I realised he was dead."

Ballybeg Prim (Rockfield Era — Ballybeg Pride) repeated Yanka Boy's Irish St Leger–Cesarewitch double in 1975. Sammy Easton, the well-known agent, bought the dog for John Bullen, an English scrapdealer.

"The dog came here for a week and then they decided they wanted him over in England," says Ger. "I was over in England at the time and I went to see him — and bejasus I didn't know him!"

McKenna got the dog back and won the 1975 Irish St Leger with him in 30.44 to become the trainer's fastest ever winner of the classic. He went on to win the Guinness 600 at Shelbourne Park in the same year and repeated his success the following year, as well as claiming the Cesarewitch. His record provokes the comment:

"He was big; a great looker," says Ger. "He was an honest-to-goodness greyhound."

There are parallels between Ballybeg Prim and Red Rasper. Both were owned by John Bullen and, again, it was decided that Red Rasper (Own Pride — Miss Honeygar) would be based in Britain. McKenna had first spotted the dog in Limerick where he did 29.56. He won a couple of races in Dublin and then the dog was taken away. He did nothing in England and then retraced Ballybeg Prim's steps back to Borrisokane — and an Irish St Leger victory in 31.15. Red Rasper did not establish himself as one of the greats in his short career. In anyone else's hands he would be anonymous; another also-ran in the history of greyhound racing. With Ger McKenna he found immortality as a classic winner.

Ger with Monalee Expert and Freddie Warrell with Ballymaclune at White City.

Owen with 1974 Irish Puppy Derby winner Shamrock Point at Harold's Cross.

CHAPTER FIVE

English Derby

W HEN Ger McKenna goes out to buy a greyhound, he looks for "a good all-round dog", bearing all competitions in mind. But primarily he is buying for the English Derby. For McKenna, it is the pivot around which the rest of the calendar revolves and it has become his own personal religion. His annual pilgrimage to White City began in 1974 and in the McKenna style, he has left his own indelible mark on the classic. He had to wait until 1981 for his first Derby winner at White City and then in 1989 he made history, becoming the first trainer to achieve a Derby double at two tracks when Lartigue Note stormed to victory at Wimbledon. But there must have been moments, many moments, when McKenna despaired of winning the English Derby. In 1974 he had a team which would compare with any generation.

It included the Yanka Boy litter brothers Ballymaclune and Ballyroughan, bred by Ignatius Kelly out of his reliable brood bitch Kitty True, and Ballykilty, which was by Always Proud. Ballymaclune and Ballyroughan had only just qualified at Limerick when McKenna took them into his care. After preparatory races at the Market's Field and Shelbourne Park, Ballymaclune was sent to Cork where he won the Guinness Trophy. Ballyroughan was directed to Shelbourne Park and made it to the final of the Easter Cup, only to break a hock. McKenna was left with Ballymaclune as his main hope for the 1974 English Derby. There were no excuses in the final won by Jimsun.

"My dog drew trap six in the final and went exceptionally wide," says Ger. "He must have been eight lengths in front at one stage. There was no saying that he was unlucky. He just threw it away by going so wide."

Bad luck certainly played a part in the 1975 classic. McKenna's representative was Shamrock Point and the dog was looking in good form as he went into the semi-finals. The competition was tough, it included Lively Band the winner of two major Irish Classics — the Derby and the St Leger. He was trained by Corkman Jack Murphy. His background was not unlike that of McKenna and he came from the rural Ireland of the same generation. He was from a large family and his early passions were horses and horse racing. Jack had been training a "dog or two" in England and on his return to Ireland took out a trainer's licence with the then recently appointed Bord na gCon. Murphy, who was to put Kilmessan, Co. Meath, on the map by turning out a succession of winners, bought Lively Band at twelve months from breeder Larry Clancy. His autobiography *Never Venture — Never Win*, which was published in 1987 just before his death from Motor Neurone Disease, relates:

"From the very beginning Lively Band, or Teddy as we called him, showed immense promise, winning at Navan in fast times when only fifteen months old.

"Naturally, he was the subject of favourable mentions in the widely read weekly edition of *The Sporting Press*, as a result of which I was approached by Matt Bruton acting on behalf of Scottish bank manager Cyril Young, who raced under the alias of Cyril Scotland. I finally accepted Matt's offer of £2,500 with a contingency of a further £1,000 to be paid to me in the event of the dog winning either the English or Irish Derby. Having bought him for £300, it was hard to refuse such a good profit — a lot of money thirteen years ago."

Lively Band was sent to Wembley trainer Tommy Johnston but showed disappointing form and seemed prone to cramp. But he regained his old sparkle just as the 1974 English Derby approached. He was eliminated at the semi-final stage but romped away with the consolation on final night at White City, the same night that Jimsun was coming from behind Ballymaclune in the Derby proper. Within days, Lively Band had been returned to Murphy who trained him to win the 1974 Carrolls' Irish Derby in an exceptionally fast 29.11. He went immediately to the International 525 at Dundalk, but the hare stopped with Lively Band several lengths clear and he made no show in the re-run. Murphy never wanted the dog to go in the re-run; nor did he wish him to go to Scotland for the Edinburgh Cup, which was being staged over the next few days. But the owner insisted and Lively Band went to the final where he finished third with Cyril Scotland's Lady Devine taking runner-up spot. Lady Devine then went to the Irish Oaks final and won the English equivalent. Lively Band was finally given the rest, which Murphy reckoned he needed so badly and he came back to take the Irish St Leger. The dual classic winner was then put to stud where he mated thirty-four bitches.

His racing career, however, was far from over. He was brought back into training and a week after he beat the great Peruvian Style at Dundalk, he was packed off again to the White City. What followed is one of the most controversial incidents in the history of greyhound racing. The greyhounds were just turning into the home straight at White City, neck and neck, when Lively Band, trained by Jack Murphy, turned his head and fought with Shamrock Point, trained by Ger McKenna.

Murphy candidly recalls that Lively Band: "fought with his challenger, leaving the stewards no option other than the immediate disqualification of my dog. I was feeling shattered by the ignominy of my dog's behaviour when insult was added to injury by the unrepeatable comments hurled at me by a rough element of the White City punters, and I was glad to reach the comparative safety of the kennel area."

Jack Murphy and Ger McKenna, two men whose every waking moment centred on greyhounds and greyhound racing, whose lives and fortunes were inseparable from those of the dogs they handled, faced one another in the paddock.

McKenna recalls: "Jack Murphy was crying. 'I'm sorry, Ger,' was all he could say."

Writing on the matter years later, and still trying to analyse what went wrong, Murphy suggested that Lively Band was such a keen greyhound, he possibly always had the potential to fight. There is a fine line between keenness and aggression, Murphy contended. Many would agree with the trainer that his hectic stint at stud could have been a contributory factor to Lively Band's misdemeanour. The fact that Lively Band was disqualified from taking any further part in the English Derby, did not stop the commotion at White City. He had finished third with Shamrock Point fourth and most of those present assumed that McKenna's dog would be automatically promoted into the final. Much the same had happened in 1968 when the Duke of Edinburgh's Camira Flash went through to the decider on a disqualification. He went on to win the final. But most did not realise that the rule had changed since the Duke's dog. It still stands today: if a qualifier is subsequently disqualified, there is a vacant trap in the showpiece. So it was in 1975, and the vociferous protests and threats of injunctions and legal action, came to nothing. As if to prove a point, Shamrock Point came out and ran away with the consolation. The Irish Puppy Derby winner two years previously, he carved his own niche in greyhound racing history when he again won the consolation event to the English Derby in 1976.

Incidentally, during that spell as a sire, Lively Band produced the subsequent English Derby winner Balliniska Band, Linacre and Ceili Band, sire of McKenna's Irish Laurels winner Rugged Mick, in just one litter. He also sired Micklem Drive, dam of English Derby winner Whisper Wishes. He later went to stud in Australia for three years but, following a decision to return him to Jack Murphy, the dog was found dead in his crate when the flight arrived in London.

McKenna looked in prime position to achieve his English Derby ambition in 1976 when he fielded the brilliant Ballybeg Prim. In the previous year the dog had enjoyed a trophy laden season, claiming the St Leger, the Cesarewitch and the Guinness 600 among his triumphs. He was brought back into training with the English Derby as his main objective and reached the final, rated the 4-5 favourite. This time it was the Philip Rees trained Mutts Silver who stole the race, beating Ballybeg Prim by 2¼ lengths. Undaunted, the Borrisokane trainer kept up his search for the greyhound who would win Britain's Blue Riband, honing his training methods to achieve the perfect preparation.

"I am looking for a good starter," says McKenna. "A good early-paced dog. September is about the latest I would want to get him, and if I consider he is good enough, I would not race him until the following season. I don't like running dogs that I think something about in the winter. During the winter months they will be half-fit through walking and galloping. We always start them off in the new season with three or four sprints before considering a race over 525 yards; and they will only race over that distance when I am happy that they are going to stay. You usually have a good idea about them being able to stay from

Ballybeg Prim, trap two, competing in Greyhound Derby trials at White City in 1975. The dog finished runner-up in the 1976 decider.

what you see in the sprints and from their breeding. But you want to go easy. There are an awful lot of races left behind at trial tracks, at the gallops and with all this road-walking. Freshness is an essential. I would give the first sprint at the end of February and it might be April before the dog's first 525. A dog could have just four races — three sprints and a 525 before Wimbledon and while it might not appear to be a lot, it is enough. If I had my way, I would be only sprinting them immediately before the English Derby, too. But you are required to trial over the full distance, so you have to do it. But in the end, win or lose, you still have a fresh dog come the end of June. He may have run right through the English Derby but he will be able to go on to Dundalk for the International 525, to Shelbourne Park for the Irish Derby and Limerick for the Irish St Leger. That is because you have not pushed him too much early on."

Parkdown Jet, the McKenna representative in 1981, obviously fitted the English Derby bill.

"You really don't have to be that exact about where you run them early on," says Ger. "My own preferences are for Shelbourne Park or Tralee, but it depends on where a suitable race comes up and there are not always that many sprint races available. Most times it is just a question of giving them race experience. It is not crucial if they don't win. Parkdown Jet had three races in Cork.He won in 29.85, 29.35 and 29.00. So we knew how good he was from an early stage. He was a good, big, strong, dog. We reckoned he would easily get 550 yards and, at the same time, he had a smashing bit of early."

The line-up for the final that year was worthy of the classic.

There was Rahan Ship (Rail Ship — Rwanyena) trained outside Dublin by Johnny Haynes whose accent was pure cockney; Geoff de Mulder's Prince Spy (Peruvian Style — Dainty Beauty); Barleyfield (Itsachampion — Bawnogue Ivy) trained by Joe Kelly; Clohast Flame (Glen Rock — Clohast Sovereign), one of a succession of finalists to be sent out by John Honeysett; In Flight (Sandman — Maythorn Pride) whose trainer Matt O'Donnell from Killenaule, Co. Tipperary, was generally regarded in Ireland as heir apparent to McKenna's classic crown; and then there was Parkdown Jet (Cairnville Jet — Gabriel Ruby). They bet 4-5 Parkdown Jet, 2-1 Rahan Ship, 7-2 Clohast Flame, 14-1 Barleyfield and 33-1 the other pair.

The view on the ground was that Parkdown Jet had a definite edge, being the only runner seeded wide, but this was contradicted by those who felt that McKenna had misjudged his preparation. Parkdown Jet had recorded a track record of 29.09 for the 500 metres in the semi-finals. He had peaked too soon, they contended. In that way, which is one of the fascinations of greyhound racing, a week of speculation, argument and counter-argument, was condensed into less than thirty seconds. The final evokes two distinct pictures. One is of Rahan Ship vaulting over one of the up-ended victims of the first bend melee, the other is of Parkdown Jet skipping around the outside, almost disdainful of his floored opponents. There were no track records. Parkdown Jet came home in 29.57, his nearest rival at the finish was 33-1 shot Prince Spy, whose owner Mrs Grace Costello, was to figure so tragically in the 1987 Irish Derby. But now the agonising disappointments of Ballymaclune and Ballybeg Prim were forgotten. Ger McKenna had finally won the English Derby and that hot summer of 1981 had had a classic ending.

There was still plenty of running left in the handsome blue dog and

The face of young Owen says it all after Parkdown Jet's win.

Morans Beef and Back Garden reach the semi-finals of the 1984 Derby.

Ger with Bold Rabbit, semi-finalist in the 1988 classic.　　　　*Amphlett*

McKenna had high hopes of giving him a chance in the Irish Derby. But a toe injury put paid to that and so he was given a lay-off.

"He went to stud, but he was so fresh," says McKenna. "Remember, the White City final was only his ninth race in all — so we decided to have a go the next season. He went straight to England after a couple of sprint gallops at the schooling track at Dunaskeagh.

"Unlike other dogs, he had the race experience, so there was no need to put him through his paces again. He went to the semi-finals in his second year. He was a marvellous dog and in great shape when he did a toe in the semi-finals. You know, of all the dogs I have ever had, I reckon that he was the one capable of winning the Derby twice."

Sport does not remember its losers, no matter how close they come. That is Ger McKenna's contention — and there are few who would dispute it. It is easily recalled that Whisper Wishes won the last running of the English Derby at White City in 1984. Readily forgotten is the fact that it was only by three-parts of a length that Moran's Beef, trained by McKenna, was denied that special place in history. We all stand guilty of the crime. We write all sorts of repetitive superlatives to describe a Derby final. The occasion and the racing public demand it. They want to be part of something *big* — not just an ordinary night. We say it was the greatest Derby of all time; the winner was the fastest greyhound ever. We build it up for the sake of the promoters, for the sake of the sponsors, which in turn is for the sake of the game. Even if the occasion is not that great after all; we are still caught up in the conspiracy. If we are not churning out the superlatives for the promoters, the sponsors, or the game, then it is for the sake of the breeder, the owner, or the trainer. But they cannot all be the greatest, these Derby finals, as much as all Ger McKenna greyhounds cannot be the greatest. In fact, some Derbies and some dogs were anything but.

The English Derby of 1984 had to be special, no matter what the result was. With just one exception — G.R. Archduke's 1940 win at Harringay — the English Derby had always been staged at White City. Now it would all end on June 23, 1984. White City was to close, although when it came, few were prepared for its sudden and cynical demise. Say what you will, it would never be the same. Which ever dog that won, would be the last winner of a Greyhound Derby at White City. That was it. The title. And it mattered. It mattered so much that it is the suffix that forever attaches to Whisper Wishes. When he is dead, the obituary will read: *Whisper Wishes — the last greyhound to win the English Derby at White City.* It made him. When everything else is forgotten, a goodish time of 29.43, a three-way photo-finish. When all this is forgotten, they will remember Whisper Wishes.

They went in trap order: Jim Wood's bitch House of Hope (Pat Seamur — Fearless Speed); Matt O'Donnell's Spartacus (Knockrour Slave — I'm A Star), later to be an Irish Derby finalist; George Curtis's The Jolly Norman (Knockrour Brandy — Breeze Valley) which, like House of Hope, was British-bred; Charlie Coyle's Whisper Wishes (Sandman — Micklem Drive); Ger McKenna's Moran's Beef (Noble Brigg — Rathkenny Bride); Francis Murray's Proud Dodger (Brave Bran — Lady Peg). They bet — 7-4 Whisper Wishes, 9-4 Moran's Beef, 9-2 Spartacus, 7-1 Proud Dodger, 12-1 House of Hope, 20-1 The Jolly Norman.

They all deserved success — House of Hope which was representing the small man; Spartacus and The Jolly Norman whose trainers no one would begrudge a Derby win. But when the traps went up there was this black streak, almost leaping with his massive propulsion, thundering right down the middle of the track. So like some of his great sons, Grove Whisper and Bold Rabbit, which Mckenna would later train. All eyes were fixed on him as he accelerated off the second bend, his great loping stride bringing him nearer to glory with every second, every metre. Suddenly a dog appeared on the outside of the pursuing pack, his right legs, fore and aft, looking ungainly, like yachtsmen leaning over to balance their craft. His feet dug into the turf, trying to correct the body's course. He drifted wide as they turned for home. Now turning straight with all legs firmly on the ground, Moran's Beef summoned up one last desperate effort against the tiring Whisper Wishes, as if they both knew exactly where the winning line was; athletes with desperation written all over disfigured faces. Even though a third runner, Proud Dodger, had come into shot, all eyes focused in those last split seconds on the two that really mattered. Then it was over. They called for proof from the camera, but we all knew that Whisper Wishes had prevailed over Moran's Beef.

"He lost by going wide at the last bend," says McKenna. The verdict was three parts of a length.

Tony Brennan had bought the dog in Tralee and McKenna went to meet him in Limerick for the collection. His first race in Shelbourne

Owen and John with the 1988 McKenna team for the English Derby at Wimbledon — January Jack, Ballinoe Linda, Lisadell Tom, Dandy Duke, Slipalong Slippy, Old Sloucher and Bold Rabbit.

Park was spectacular. He won in 29.39.

"That was when everything else was doing 30.50," McKenna adds.

Moran's Beef was going to be a little bit different. We knew that from the start. There was that 29.39 — and the fact that he was not down to Brennan or McKenna.

"There's no use in telling you a lie," says McKenna. "There was a mix-up when he was being renamed. There was a dog and a bitch and there was a mistake when the dog was put down to some fella Gerry Moran. I heard later he was a butcher in Dublin, hence Moran's Beef . . . or, come to think of it, was he an accountant or something . . ."

Moran's Beef ran in the Produce Stakes and McKenna never had any intention of bringing him to White City.

"He was far too novicey. But Tony Brennan said he could get him at 40-1, so could I bring him with my other dogs, Count Five and Lauragh Six."

It is fair to say that when the changeover came, Wimbledon fooled everyone. The general view was that new 480 metres distance would be comparatively easy. The track had moved the winning line to extend the standard distance from 460 metres, making it more compatible with the recognised Derby distance. Its tight turns and fast sand surface were expected to suit the short runner. It was a misconception shared by all. Rugged Mick ran there in the Daily Mirror Anglo-Irish International and blew up by the third bend. Wimbledon was not all that it seemed. Ger McKenna had not intended to bring back Moran's Beef for a second tilt at the English classic, but now he thought otherwise.

"It was really only an afterthought. Tony Brennan had reservations but in the end he said: 'Whatever you think, Boss.' "

McKenna was alone among Irish trainers in recognising the requirements of Wimbledon. It was an inspired move to bring Moran's Beef: "He loved the place," said Ger. Moran's Beef quickly established himself as favourite, went to the quarter-finals and shattered his wrist at the first bend. It had taken McKenna a veritable lifetime and a generation of great greyhounds to finally secure an English Derby at White City. Wimbledon had already given him notice that it would be no easier to conquer.

The build-up to the English Derby starts early and an integral part of the pre-competition fever is finding out which dogs McKenna is bringing over. In 1989 all eyes were on Lodge Dancer, quoted as the pre-season ante-post favourite. Attractive Son and Lartigue Note made up his trio of entries. But it was the little known black dog by One To Note that reached the classic final.

It was a big night for Ireland, not spoiled by success in the international sporting arena. Ger McKenna was fielding not only a finalist but the favourite in the Blue Riband decider. And if Pat O'Donovan, producer with Radio Telefis Eireann (RTE) Ireland's national radio and television network, was worried that he would be troubled to fill in that gap between the 9.15pm start of transmission and the 10.25pm off-time of the Derby, he did not have an anxious moment. They queued up only too happily, the dozens who had something to tell: My Part In The Rise and Rise of Lartigue Note. The barometer rose above 80 degrees Fahrenheit and made the diners in the Wimbledon restaurant wish that someone would remove his bow tie so that they could follow suit and not feel conspicuous. Outside, at least, there was a slight breeze wafting around the limited area from which the radio broadcast was being made. It was 10 o'clock and over three hours since the night's programme began.

Trumpets sounded and raucous roars of excitement filled the night air. The dogs were coming out on parade for the final. Those on the official side straightened their dickie bows and fingered their collars, allowing their necks to taste the sweet coolness of the breeze, such as it was. And there he prances down the steps, his white shirt open, his sleeves rolled up. Himself. Totally at ease. You could imagine him strolling down the strand at Ballybunion on a summer's afternoon, a dog by the lead. For him there was no dress code. I recalled how one journalist in 1981 had remarked in print how McKenna had gone to the winner's rostrum wearing a blue suit and brown shoes. An irrelevance.

"And who are you?"

"And now we have Tom Moore from Ballybunion in the County of Kerry, breeder of the favourite Lartigue Note."

The voice, unmistakable to listeners to RTE radio, was that of Miceal O'Muircheartaigh. Eight years earlier Tom Moore could never have believed that he would be standing here at the nerve centre. Quite detached from what was going on, he had watched Parkdown Jet's win on the television in the living room in Ballybunion. There are a thousand breeders in Ireland who hope that some day someone will call and express an interest in a pup and say they are representing someone who might or might not be Eddie Costello, who wants to buy the animal. That happened to others; not Tom Moore. Just like the National Lottery. The odds are staggering. It would be years later before Fate would point Tom Moore down the same road. He bought Lartigue Sooty, a decent dog which would later be trained in England by Geoffrey de Mulder. Lartigue Sooty was by Killaclug Jet out of Gabriel Doll. Tom Moore liked the dog but felt he would like a Gabriel Doll whelp by a different sire. He scanned The Sporting Press week after week. He finally found that Gabriel Doll had a litter to Echo Spark. So it was that Lartigue Spark (Echo Spark — Gabriel Doll) was brought to One To Note, a dog that had been the victim of a massive pile-up in the penultimate stage of the 1984 English Derby. It was enough to ruin his chances in the classic, but he took the Consolation Stakes in his stride.

On an oppressively hot June evening in 1989, Tom Moore, his chest expanded, watched Owen McKenna, son of the trainer, give a reassuring pat to Lartigue Note, a son of the luckless One To Note out of Lartigue Spark, a daughter of Gabriel Doll, on the way to traps for the final of the English Derby at Wimbledon amid an ever rising din. Just as an older McKenna had done with Parkdown Jet all those years before at White City. Here was Fate. Here was Coincidence. Here was Ger McKenna in the final with Lartigue Note, whose grandam Gabriel Doll was a litter sister of Parkdown Jet. Ger McKenna was unaware of the connection. Unaware of the connection right up to when somebody told him weeks after the Derby decider. It certainly never crossed his mind on an evening in Limerick as he washed the feet of Grove Whisper. If McKenna's encyclopaedic knowledge of his trade and its raw material falls down on any point it is breeding. He seldom refers to it because he is not as authoritative as others on the matter. Not that he cares. Greyhounds are assessed on their own ability. Not what their antecedents achieved. Now Grove Whisper *had* ability. The experienced tracker, winner of the Shelbourne leg of the Anglo-Irish International and track record holder at Limerick had just run a trial in 29.66 for Limerick's 525 yards. There was one more trial before racing and McKenna had not left the track before the result was in, 29.87. The winner was 14 months old. McKenna departed the scene not so much with Grove Whisper in hand but the yardstick by which a future champion would be gauged. It is not just rivals and friends who talk in awe of Ger McKenna. His family does too.

John McKenna, eldest of the trainer's three sons said: "He came home and told us he had found a Derby winner. He bought the dog for Cathal McCarthy but then he just left it to lie in the kennels. We wondered what was going on, what he was going to do with him."

The dog's itinerary, when he finally resumed racing, seemed directionless. A hotch-potch of races at Lifford in the far north, Dublin's Shelbourne Park of course — and Thurles and Waterford. McKenna is put in an unenviable position when he finds a potential winner. If he tips one owner off, then others are bound to be upset. Such is life. In this case, history records that McKenna got in touch with McCarthy when Lartigue Note surfaced. The owner saw his new hope in the early days. McKenna rang him when the dog was due to run at Shelbourne Park. The trainer suggested he bring some money. They went for a 'touch'. Lartigue Note was knocked over at the first of the two bends in the sprint race. Not an auspicious start. As a Greyhound

Correspondent, I ring Ger McKenna regularly. So much so that I never refer to the directory, I press the telephone digits automatically.

"Hang on. He's over in the yard," says Josie.

"Well . . ." within minutes McKenna is on the phone, and happy to talk. There is something which I have always found peculiar in Ger McKenna. Greyhound racing seems to lend itself to covertness, but McKenna shuns such secrecy.

"Ger fancies this one; Ger doesn't fancy this one," you hear alternatively at the races.

With other trainers, it is usually just hearsay. But with Ger McKenna, the chances are that they have asked Ger himself . . . and he has told them.

"I've an old dog here that I think will win the English Derby. He's a big price. You could do worse than have a few bob on him."

Lartigue Note was 66-1 that day. On May 28, after winning his preliminary round of the English Derby in 28.69, he would be only 6-1 to survive four more rounds and win the final. Survival was the operative word, next time out. He squeezed through in third place behind Ard Knock in the First Round proper and there were anxious moments in the semi-final, too, before he ran up to Catsrock Rocket. In between, there were best-of-the-night runs of 28.50 and 28.60 for the 480 metres. But even in defeat — especially in defeat — McKenna had seen enough to buoy his confidence.

"I knew he had the pace. Those losses showed that he had the heart and determination, too."

McKenna's faith was undiminished even when the trap draw for the final put Lartigue Note — now a confirmed trap one specialist — in trap two with Castleivy Mick — observed running off the rails at the penultimate stage — on his inner. The other four were wide seeds.

McKenna puts it quite simply: "I said to Owen: If he can't beat Castleivy Mick to the bend, then we have no right being here."

Personally, I had never seen the great man so self-assured.

A long week came to an end at 6.45 on Saturday, June 24. The traps went up and the Daily Mirror Kennel Championship final was run. The Derby night programme was underway. The most often heard complaint from those not conversant with the sport of greyhound racing is that it is all over so quickly. A flash and it's on to the next race. But for those with an involvement, however peripheral, in the glamour

Lartigue Note in full flight.   *Steve Nash*

Celebrations following Lartigue Note's victory.   *Steve Nash*

event on the calendar, the final of the English Derby, the waiting is unbearable. The pressure is still greater for those connected with the favourite. There is that bit more to live up to. That bit more to lose. You search for encouraging signs. There are none. Dogs beaten by Lartigue Note in earlier rounds fail to maintain their form and compliment his. The supplementary races pass and the Invitation Stakes, race nine, sees Lartigue Note's kennel companion Attractive Son fail to catch Ard Knock. And then, quite suddenly, such comparisons of performance seem irrelevant. Race ten is over. Now only time separates us from the occasion we have all come to witness. The runners file past the Judge's box, the Sky TV cameras, the RTE radio microphones; all congregated in an inadequate few square feet. But the proximity, the heat, and the chants of the crowd all lend to the tension and the atmosphere. All questions about whether Wimbledon is the correct choice as venue for the Derby are meaningless. Here and now it is the Mecca. Close your eyes and it is White City eight years ago.

They go by in trap order: Castleivy Mick (Moral Support — Rambling Florist) (Greenacre, Unattached); Lartigue Note (One To Note — Lartigue Spark) (McKenna, Ireland); Cooladine Style (Easy And Slow — Cooladine Dove) (Stringer, Norton Canes); Catsrock Rockct (Lauragh Six — Busy Bubble) (O'Hare, Unattached); Early Vocation (Manorville Sand — Chick Luck) (Honeysett, Wembley); Kilcannon Bullet (Odell Supreme — Murlen's Toe) (Coleman, Walthamstow). They are all attached to an owner who longs to be handed the trophy and see his name forever in the sporting annals; to the breeder who regarded the pup almost as his or her own child, rearing it, educating it, feeding it, healing its wounds, watching its young bones and mischievous character develop; to the trainer who depends on the dog's success to further strengthen his or her reputation and kennel; to the kennelhand who will never stand in the limelight; to the punter with a betting slip clasped in a sweaty palm; to a nation back home, the communal ear cocked to the radio. They bet: Evens Lartigue Note, 2-1 Kilcannon Bullet, 7-1 Catsrock Rocket, 10-1 Castleivy Mick, Early Vocation, 25-1 Cooladine Style.

A blue blur and it's all over. Lartigue Note — the erratic starter, the confirmed trap one runner — is out in front. Off the second bend. This is where he really comes into his own. Go. Go. Go. A quick look behind. The others are struggling. But so much can go wrong. Keep going.

Keep going. Lartigue Note turns for home in glorious isolation. A few more strides and it will be all over. Arms raised. He crosses the line.

"I said to Owen: If we can't beat Castleivy Mick to the bend then we have no right being here," Ger had said.

It seemed that the whole of County Tipperary, the whole of Ireland was at Plough Lane. *It's A Long Way To Tipperary*, they sang, amid scenes never before witnessed at an English Derby final. Owen was swamped, the dog in one hand, the Tipperary flag in the other, the grin on his cherubic face never wider. Ger, his jacket abandoned, stood there in tie, striped shirt and braces, his glasses held on by what would later be described as bootlaces, dispensing his autograph.

Ger McKenna Superstar.

CHAPTER SIX

The Irish Derby

TOM Hayes is a person not given to hyperbole. A tall, gentle, distinguished-looking man, the wealthy Killaloe, Co. Clare, builder's tones are soft and not given to excitement. His words and thoughts are studied. Tom Hayes does not jump in. He was the man who gave the Irish Coursing Club a new respectability in the mid-eighties when, after a traumatic period, he assumed the role of treasurer. In successive years, the ICC returned record profits. When Tom Hayes pronounces Ger McKenna as: "probably the greatest greyhound trainer ever," it means something. Hayes adds: "I have never known a trainer to pay so much attention to detail; to sacrifice so much in personal time for the sake of his dogs."

In between administering various aspects of the ICC and his successful business life, Tom Hayes is no mean trainer himself. In fact, on the coursing field he has had few peers. But 1969 stands out as one of the supreme achievements in the sport when with Tender Heather, Tender Honey and Tender Hero, Tom Hayes won the Coursing Derby and Oaks at Clonmel and the Irish Cup at Clounanna.

"We ran Tender Heather at Finnoe where he was beaten just up in the second round. We did not run him again until Abbeyfeale where he won the trial stake. Truthfully, we never realised how good he was until he won the Derby in Clonmel." Tender Heather was hurt in Corn na Gaillimhe at the Galway and Oranmore fixture as an all-age and his career was over. But it was just the start for the Ger McKenna-trained dog that had beaten him as a puppy at Finnoe. McKenna was secretary of that coursing club and, as any one in that position will testify, it is an onerous job. You invariably have either too many entries or not enough.

In the 1968/69 season, McKenna was stuck. In desperation, he put in a dog which had been sent to him by Tom O'Doherty, a Cree, Co. Clare publican and farmer.

"It was not unusual, because most track dogs coursed in those days," says Ger. "Nowadays track greyhounds are regarded as being too valuable to risk up a field."

Still, the presumption would be that the pure coursing dog would prevail in any match. McKenna's dog won a round and then just out-paced his opponent in the second round. The beaten dog was coursing classic winner-to-be Tender Heather. The winning dog, trained by Finnoe Coursing Club secretary Ger McKenna, was Own Pride. It is, perhaps, little wonder that Own Pride upset Tender Heather.

"He was the most determined greyhound I ever handled," says Ger. "He would go through that wall there. He'd follow anything."

McKenna was still trying to gauge the greyhound's ability at this point. Tom O'Doherty had just rung him up and asked him to take "a dog". "That's the way they did it in those days," says Ger. He sent Own Pride home for the winter and the dog had filled out nicely on his return. McKenna soon knew that he had something special. He recalls one race particularly well. McKenna asked Jimmy Kinihan, then the track manager at Kilkenny and later a firm friend, to put the dog into a race. McKenna's impish smile must have betrayed a certain cockiness, for Kinihan, rated by McKenna as one of the all-time great judges of a greyhound, replied: "Why? Do you think I can't beat him?" Kinihan was well capable of beating the shrewdest trainer, as McKenna recounts: "If he thought you were a certainty, he would put you in trap three with a wide runner on your inside and a railer on your outside." There was no malice. It was a game; a battle of wits. Like most good natured jousts of its kind, this one ended in a draw.

"I hope Kinihan is in heaven," says Ger. "I thought the world of him. But, boy, he was a whore." The money was down and the diminutive McKenna paraded the dog himself. Own Pride had drawn four, or Kinihan had given him four — according to which way you like to look at it. True to form, he had a wide runner in three and a railer in five. Stuck in the in-field, McKenna could not quite make out the finish. But it was close. Both men had proved a point. It was a dead-heat in 30.30.

Own Pride's Derby preparation started with the Midland Puppy

Owner Deirdre Hynes, watched by her mother, receives the trophy from Mrs Des Ryan after Bashful Man had won the 1973 Carroll's Irish Derby at Shelbourne Park. Ger and Josie are joined on the left by Seamus Flanagan, Chief Officer, Bord na gCon.

Ger and owner Tom O'Docherty after Own Pride had won the 1969 Irish Derby at Harold's Cross.

Stake at Mullingar. Own Pride (Always Proud — Kitty True) ran a fast 29.59 at Mullingar, but that feature went to Monalee Gambler. At Harold's Cross, he showed gradual improvement, to make his way to the head of the market for the final of the 1969 Irish Derby, the last to be run at Harold's Cross. But Monalee Gambler was still there in the decider. The pair dominated the final with Monalee Gambler getting first run, but Own Pride came to take it up at the third bend and went on to win comfortably in 29.20. It was Ger McKenna's first Derby and Own Pride had made history. He was the fastest ever winner of the premier classic in the years that it was run at Harold's Cross. He was the only greyhound to interrupt Tender Heather's march to the coursing Derby and he became the sixth link in McKenna's great chain of Irish St Leger winners when he broke thirty-one seconds in the classic final at Limerick.

In 1970, the Irish Derby was transformed. Cigarette company P.J. Carroll had become its first sponsor and it had found a permanent home at Shelbourne Park. But some things had not changed. Own Pride was back, trying to become the first greyhound since Spanish Battleship to win the classic in successive years. The decider provided the last great Derby confrontation in the Ger McKenna-Gay McKenna-Tom Lynch triangle as Menelaus was to be Tom Lynch's last finalist in the showpiece. Gay was to win the day, with Monalee Pride popping out to lead all the way. Own Pride moved into the second but had been carrying a shoulder injury all week and could make no impression on the winner. They passed the line in that order: Gay McKenna-Ger McKenna-Tom Lynch.

Ger says of Own Pride's valiant double bid: "In any other circumstances, I would have withdrawn him because of the injury. But since it was the Derby final, we let him take his chance. He was not the fastest of dogs. But there were none more honest."

Sole Aim took honours in the 1971 Irish Derby and his owner Mrs Frances Chandler can thus be included in that select band of owners whose name has been attached to two Derby winners. This member of the famous London-based greyhound family had won the Irish Derby of twenty years earlier with Carmody's Tanist. Time Up Please made it to the finals of the '71 Derby and reached the semi-finals in the following year, but Ger's main hopes rested with one of his personal favourites. It was Eamon Gayner's Ballykilty, who got the wide draw he so badly needed in the decider. But the race did not go as was anticipated. Ballykilty came away well, but lost enough ground at the corner to effectively hand the race to Catsrock Daisy, trained by cousin Gay. Cyril Scotland was on his way to emulating Mrs Chandler, as he owned Catsrock Daisy in partnership with Matt Bruton, and then acquired the 1974 Irish Derby winner Lively Band. Ballykilty had at least left his mark. The twenty-nine second barrier was breached by Prince of Bermuda with his track record of 28.98 in 1956 and by the time Ballykilty had finished, it was down to 28.80.

Bashful Man (Myross Again — Ballyflake) was bought out of Youghal from a seed and wool merchant from Carrigtwohill, Co. Cork, Michael O'Dwyer. The new owner was Deirdre Hynes whose family were hoteliers at Portumna, Co. Galway, just seven miles out of the road from Borrisokane. If there is such a thing as a lucky owner then Deirdre Hynes just about fitted the bill. She also owned the Ger McKenna-trained Irish Cesarewitch and Guinness 600 winner Itsachampion and later found more fame with Peruvian Style, trained in her hometown by Tony Fahy. Bashful Man was bought just six months before the Irish Derby. But it was only when he shaped well in an open race against Larry Kelly's great bitch Romping To Work that McKenna realised that he had an above average performer. Romping To Work won the Irish Oaks that year and broke twenty-nine seconds at Harold's Cross in the process. She started her Derby campaign with a 29.05 run and the form of the earlier open race worked out well when Bashful Man did 29.13. McKenna was also fielding Ballymaclune, a near-relation of Ballykilty and Own Pride. But amid the usual ups and down of the Derby, it was Bashful Man which emerged as a clear favourite with a 29.01 run in the quarter-finals and 29.15 success at the penultimate stage. The 1973 Derby final — which carried a prize of £10,000 thanks to Carrolls' sponsorship — was extraordinary not just for the winning time of 28.82, but because Bashful Man came from behind and then held off a proven stayer in Gay McKenna's Irish Cesarewitch winner Rita's Choice. Little did those present realise that the time would be written indelibly into the record books, never to be bettered in an Irish Derby final. In 1986, with the record still intact, the Irish Derby distance was extended to 550 yards. Bashful Man's Achilles Heel was his dislike of heavy going. He followed Time Up Please by winning the International 525 at Dundalk, but a water-logged Limerick could not be conquered in the Irish St Leger. "When Limerick gets heavy, it's a bog," says McKenna. "It was all against Bashful Man, something like .75 slow. But he was a good all-round dog." The ground was sticky on the night that he was beaten by Romping To Work at Shelbourne Park in the pre-Derby race which so impressed his trainer. When the ground improved, so did Bashful Man.

There is a sad postscript to the career of Bashful Man. He died en route to Australia where he was being exported for a new life at stud.

The luckless Shamrock Point contested the Irish Derby in 1975 and he was joined by Ballybeg Prim in 1976. McKenna's Here's Tat was favourite throughout the 1977 running when the first prize had reached £20,000. But, in one of the big upsets in recent times, he could not close down the lead established by the Paddy Keane-trained Pampered Rover, and so Keane just narrowly preceded McKenna in training a winner of both the English and Irish Derby. McKenna's premier classic consistency was again evident when he got the outstanding bitch Nameless Pixie into the decider. It was a bitches year, and victory went to Penny County, trained by Matt Travers. She was only the fifth of her sex to win the dog-dominated classic. Nameless Pixie was back in the final the following year, along with Knockrour Slave, but it was the young trainer Michael Barrett who followed up his success of 1977 with Linda's Champion by producing the 1980 victor Suir Miller.

Many trainers and kennels which figured so prominently at the turn of the decade are no longer heard of; but McKenna is a stayer. They were not all great dogs but they were there when it counted. Samuel Biss's Captain Miller (Ivy Hall Solo — Crow's First) started favourite for the 1983 Irish Derby, now worth £25,000, and kennel companion Brideview Sailor (Shamrock Sailor — Blonde Exile), owned by Tony Brennan, came to within a length of beating Belvedere Bran. They were not all classic winners — but Count Five in the 1984 final gave Cathal McCarthy the appetite for the game which would only be satisfied by Lartigue Note. They were not all lucky — but Here's Negrow (Sand Man — Here's Jenny) was worthy of his place in the 1986 showdown. What thrills he gave Tony Mulgrew. They were not all fast — but Eddie Costello's Rathgallen Tady was in the right trap on an emotion-filled night in 1987.

CHAPTER SEVEN

Costello Derby

THERE is a photograph, unique in the Irish Derby gallery. Ostensibly, it is posed in standard style. A smiling sponsor hands over the trophy. But there is something not quite right. It has a strange, haunting feel. Somebody is missing. It is as if someone has put a chemical agent to the print, erasing a figure. But the result is less than perfect. It is flawed so that a shadow, evidence of the attempt, remains. Perhaps there is a clue to the incompleteness of the study. Ger McKenna stands there smiling, his wife Josie by his side. McKenna is an unwilling prop when such presentations come around. He is a reluctant model. It would have gone down as a memorable Derby, the last to be sponsored by Carrolls, only the second over 550 yards, one of the few to be decided by a photograph. Instead it was dominated by those not even there.

Eddie Costello was born in 1938. Like so many of his compatriots, Roscomman man Costello went into the building trade. A member of a smaller, elite, group — the inner circle — his exile in Britain had left him enormously wealthy. His wife Grace was a woman of extraordinary energy. Deeply involved in her husband's company, she also shared his interest in greyhounds, the ups and even more regular downs. For in greyhound racing folklore, Costello had gone down as a legendary loser.

Thirty years earlier Eddie Costello had gone to Britain fired with the ambition to make money. To be successful. To be talked about back in County Roscommon as Eddie Costello: local boy makes good. The epitaph assured, Costello was consumed by a new passion, a passion which turned into an obsession. He would win the Greyhound Derby. It was an ambition which touched those around him, too. Even if he

Eddie Costello.   *Steve Nash*

never mentioned a dog when you talked, you were conscious of just one thing — this was Eddie Costello who wanted to win the Derby. When he did, it did not matter. On a Saturday in September in Dublin, Eddie Costello won his Derby — and he didn't give a damn. "The race didn't matter to me. When I watch it on video, I am still not interested because I was not involved," he said.

Just twenty-four hours before the final to the 1987 Carrolls Irish Derby, the person most touched by Costello's Derby dream — his wife, Grace — had died.

The promise shown of an early Derby success by Eugene McNamara-trained Swibo, which won the Consolation in 1977, had no immediate fulfilment for Costello. Hurry On Bran ran up to the John Hayes-trained Indian Joe in the English Derby of 1980 at White City. Indian Joe was injured going into the race and Francis Murray, the new Costello trainer, must have been confident of an early delivery of the goods for his new, important patron. But Hurry On Bran went back to Shelbourne Park and failed in the Irish final, too. In 1981, Costello launched an all-out assault on the British Blue Riband. He purchased no fewer than eleven greyhounds to compete at White City and Costello-owned runners filled the first two places in the long-odds lists. Hurry On Bran had cost £4,500; Calandra Champ £3,500 and Murray's Mixture £5,000; but they hardly got a run. Sickeness, never actually pinpointed, devastated the Murray string. That year's Derby was sealed with devilish irony. Prince Spy, a comparatively cheap purchase and running in the name of Grace Costello and trained by Geoffrey de Mulder, went to traps for the final as one of the 33-1 outsiders. He came out of the heap which was the first bend scene and gained on the leader with every stride. But he never made it. The Irish were singing. Tipperaryman Ger McKenna had landed his first English Derby with Parkdown Jet. It was 1981 and Costello still had a long way to go.

It rained cats and dogs on the night, later that year, when Calandra Champ went off the 4-6 favourite to win the Carrolls Irish Derby. He finished second to Bold Work and the second Costello runner Brickyard Gem came in last. At this stage Costello was shelling out about £60,000 a year in purchase prices alone for dogs of Derby potential. Proud Dodger, like all Costello dogs of this era, was trained by Francis Murray. Luckless again. Proud Dodger did two toes in the semi-finals and, just as easily as we tend to forget how close Moran's

Beef got to beating Whisper Wishes, we overlook that this was a three-way photo-finish to White City's last Derby. Proud Dodger had run a blinder to finish third. Costello stuck with Murray; or was it vice versa? They were saying now that Murray was jinxed, too. Around this time, I rang the owner of a greyhound wanted by Costello. The owner explained why he had refused the proverbial open cheque: "I'd have been signing the dog's death warrant. The dog would break his leg at least." It had come to be that bad. Paranoia had set in. Moral Support was bought for over £20,000 and immediately broke his leg, never to race again.

As much as he had had the ownership of nearly all of the top dogs, Costello had already utilised three of the top trainers. But Murray, McNamara and Paddy Keane had failed in the only event that mattered to Costello. And Keane, remember, was the man, along with McKenna, who had trained winners of the Irish and English Derby: Faithful Hope in 1966 when his trainer was based at Clapton and, back in Ireland, Pampered Rover in 1978, gave the much-travelled Clareman his double niche in greyhound racing history. For some reason, we were surprised when Costello turned to McKenna. And yet, it seemed the most logical combination possible: Top trainer/leading owner. Glenbrien Champ, Lissadell Tom, Ninth Wave . . . the list was reading like a canine *"Who's Who"* — but, all came and went. We wondered if Costello had a contagious disease. Okay, let us not run away with the idea that Costello never won a race. But the Produce Stakes (Calandra Champ) and Irish Cesarewitch (Murray's Mixture) were mere morsels when one craved the main menu. The Derby.

"Ger recommended Rathgallen Tady to me and I bought the dog," said Costello. "But with Grace so ill, I was simply aware that he was in the Derby and that was all. Grace rang on the Saturday of the semi-finals to see if he had qualified, but in the end she had no sense of time and asked me that week if the dog had won the final."

During the evening of Friday, September 18, Grace Costello died. The following night, Rathgallen Tady started at 8-1 to give owner Eddie Costello his first and trainer Ger McKenna his third Irish Derby. It was ten years since Swibo had been Costello's first Derby representative and when success came he had spent £600,000 trying to win a race worth £27,500.

Eddie Costello is a "dacant man", according to McKenna. The

Proud Dodger.   *N and B Photos*

Glenbrien Champ.   *N and B Photos*

trainer likes Costello's style as an owner, paying big for the best dogs and keeping out of his side of the business. McKenna bought Rathgallen Tady for Costello after the dog had won its first race at Thurles. Only McKenna knew how unlucky they had been with Glenbrien Champ, though he stresses they were unfortunate. It was nothing to do with a jinx or anything like that, it was simply a matter of cause and effect. Rathgallen Tady ran well in Cork, but McKenna pulled him out of the competition. The trainer was learning more about his new charge: "He was an exceptionally wide runner and I knew he would take time to come to hand," he said.

McKenna had the patience. He was blessed with it. It was the familiar pattern. Winning was incidental. It was a question of giving the dog race experience. This is the tried and trusted McKenna method which has won the Irish Derby three times, the English Derby twice, the Irish St Leger twelve times, the Irish Laurels six times, the Irish Cesarewitch four times, the Irish National Sprint twice, the Produce Stakes twice and the Irish Oaks once. But McKenna must have pondered on Rathgallen Tady's ability to contribute to his classic tally.

The dog ran in a race of no significance at Tralee: "He jogged around the track for the good of his health," said McKenna. John Ward, racing manager at the Co. Kerry track, is no mean judge. He must have thought that McKenna, who had enthused about the dog, was going senile. McKenna refused to believe what he had seen. He brought him to Errill, to the schooling track outside Roscrea, Co. Tipperary, which he uses as an alternative to the bog down the road. Charismatic renewal! McKenna, a new and relieved man, pronounced: "This fellow will win the Derby — *if* he gets trap six." The conclusion was that Rathgallen Tady had simply not acted around Tralee: "It was not his track."

Sean Collins, Public Relations Officer of Bord na gCon and later elevated to the post of Chief Executive, was forced to admit that he had told a white lie. When we gathered in the Dublin hotel to hear details of the upcoming Irish Derby, Collins admitted that what he had denied earlier in the day, was true. Carrolls were pulling out of the Derby, having been its first sponsor in 1970. A sadly historic occasion. Ger McKenna, who had won the last unsponsored Derby in 1969 with Own Pride, was preparing to bridge the gap since his last Blue Riband with Bashful Man in 1973. The pressure was on; but not on the trainer.

" . . . *If* he gets six."

Bord Na gCon, in a move unpopular with racegoers and those connected with the finalists, had decided a couple of years previously that they would no longer make the draw for the final on the night of the semi-finals. Instead, the trap draw would be made by the owners on the Monday before the decider. This was an idea designed to get a degree more media coverage for the event and it all added to the tension. The race-cloths were sealed in six envelopes. The sealed envelopes were placed, willy-nilly, in six white boxes. The owner approached, chose a box, withdrew the envelope, opened the envelope. A hint of red, blue, white; and they instantly knew their fate. Josie McKenna, the trainer's attractive wife, stood in for owner Eddie Costello who was in London with his wife, who was at death's door. Josie was smiling pleasantly, laughing. As serene as ever. Inside she was knotted. She knew two things: "If I drew anything but six, we had no chance and if I drew trap one, the dog would ruin the race for the rest."

She unstuck the envelope. Afraid to look. A hint of orange. It was trap six! Only the occasion made her stifle the delight she felt inside. Josie was as proud as punch — as if she had trained the winner. "First time she ever did a right thing in her life," laughs the real trainer.

I remember not having a bet. By this stage you have met every owner and trainer involved — each nice in his or her own way. But Costello's wife has died and you want him to win this time. Above any other, this time. My money would only stop the dog. The superstitions are spreading . . .

They went to traps: Matt O'Donnell's Ardfert Sean (Easy And Slow — Kielduff Fun), Christy Daly's Randy (Aulton Villa — Melanie); Tony Meek's Gino (Ballyheigue Moon — Model Snowdrop); Ger McKenna's Balailka (Moral Support — Bondvella); Mary McCall's Carter's Lad (Linda's Champion — Carter's Lass) and Ger McKenna's Rathgallen Tady (Overdraught Pet — Mae West) They bet — 9-4 Ardfert Sean, Carter's Lad; 9-2 Randy, 5-1 Balailka, 7-1 Gino, 8-1 Rathgallen Tady.

The door of the Press Room swung open and banged against the back wall. Josie McKenna could hardly speak: "Did he get up?" she blurted. Carter's Lad and Rathgallen Tady had gone across the line in unison. To the naked eye Carter's Lad was up; but Rathgallen Tady was on the right, as the shrewd judges will tell you, near-side in the photo-finish. The psychology in such situations is intriguing. The odds heavily

Ger and Josie and son John after Rathgallen Tady had won the 1987 Irish Derby at Shelbourne Park. The previous evening, Grace Costello had died.

favoured Josie McKenna believing the worst: "I think we're beaten," she said.

What is it? I suppose it's a buffer against disappointment, a buffer against looking silly. Just in case you really are beaten. The gregarious, but infuriating, Terry McCann, another McKenna owner, is a classic. He owned the Waterloo Cup winner Tubbertelly Queen. The bitch, an outstanding winner, had it every way — on the handicap, on speed, on the working. The slips drop. They're off and running. Tubbertelly Queen away and gone. Easily. Going away. The first turn. Then another. And another. No contest. McCann, even more pot-bellied than McKenna — a non-drinking Falstaff — declares: "I think we're beaten." I thought McKenna, enjoying every twist and drive of the exhibition by his bitch, would hit him.

Now here was Josie saying the same thing. But with reason; it is desperately close. A whisker. I came back from looking at the video of the race down the corridor, and I thought Rathgallen Tady had got up. But dare I say it and risk a lifetime of ignominy for raising her hopes; just to have them dashed?

"Josie, I think you're up . . . but I can't be sure . . ."

Suddenly, silence. The announcer's voice. Like a bomb exploding on an unsuspecting town: "Result — 6 and 5 . . ." The rest is mayhem and Ger McKenna history.

CHAPTER EIGHT

The Irish Cesarewitch

"WHAT'S the delay?" I asked. The reply was quite unbelievable: "The judge is measuring the dogs' noses." It had to be one of the most bizarre nights in greyhound racing and, right enough, when history was being made — Ger McKenna was stuck right in the middle of it. And so we waited . . . and waited. In fact, a whole nation hung on the outcome. Not that they had any personal monetary interest in the outcome, but simply because they had been caught up in the fascination of the whole episode. It was one of the half-dozen nights in the year when RTE gives live television coverage to the sport and the crew got more than they bargained for — not a soccer match; but a greyhound race which had gone into extra time. On reflection, we should have anticipated such a finish to the 1986 Guinness 600, the £5,000 feature which is one of the oldest and most prestigious since sponsorship came to the game.

They lined up: Ger McKenna's Here's Negrow (Sand Man — Here's Jenny) which would later contest the Irish Derby final from the same trap; Sean Bourke's Oughter Brigg (Noble Brigg — Dromacossane) later to win the Irish Cesarewitch; Davy Lennon's Low Sail (Sail On — Low and Behold), the Guinness Irish National Sprint runner-up; Noel Kinsella's Irish Oaks runner-up Lispopple Story (Liberty Lad — Lispopple Blast); Michael Enright's Hideaway Cheeta (Hume Highway — Hideaway Girl) which had run up the Easter Cup; and Mrs Patricia Power's Odell Yankee (Sail On — Odell Sarah) which had won the Guinness Trophy at Cork. They bet: 2-1 Here's Negrow; 4-1 Oughter Brigg, Low Sail, Lispopple Story; 9-2 Odell Yankee; 10-1 Hideaway Cheeta.

With the exception of Odell Yankee, they all looked guaranteed to get the trip. But a finish like it had seldom — perhaps never — been seen at Shelbourne Park where, so often, a greyhound gets to the front and stays there. You could have thrown a blanket over the first five. The only race to match it was the 1983 Carrolls' International 525 at Dundalk when Mrs Mary McGrath's Quick Suzy beat the fifth dog by a length. And so we waited and waited . . . But there was no result. Replay followed replay on the TV screen. One minute it looked like Here's Negrow. Then a change of mind: It could be just Oughter Brigg. Suddenly, the silence was broken. Excited talk spread through the stadium. The judge was not in his box. He was heading towards the weigh room with a measuring tape. Maurice O'Riordan could not believe his eyes. The print appeared to show that Here's Negrow was just up. But could his nose be that long? There was only one way to find out. It is a popular belief that they dislike awarding dead-heats at Irish tracks. It complicates the Tote. But surely this was taking it to the giddy end. But, there he was measuring the dogs' noses! Finally, it came: Result 2–1. In fairness, the print — when publicly displayed — did appear to substantiate O'Riordan's belief that it was flawed and was not an accurate photograph. The camera had lied. The distances were a short head, a head, a neck, a neck, and 2½ lengths with Low Sail third, Lispopple Story fourth, Hideaway Cheeta fifth and Odell Yankee the only one not in the photo-finish. McKenna was not convinced:

"To this day, I still believe we got up."

"We", in this instance, meant Here's Negrow. But in a remarkable twist to the following year's Irish Cesarewitch, "We" would be Oughter Brigg, formerly trained by Sean Bourke and owned by Mossy McEllestrim of Ballyduff, Co. Kerry. There is a code which Ger McKenna has always observed right from his father's days through the time when, as a married man, he moved into a rented flat in Borrisokane and then to a rented house out the road at Tower Hill. Money was often tight, but you never poached another trainer's dog.

"I do not know what happened between the owner and his previous trainer, Sean Bourke," says Ger. "The owner just rang me and asked me to take him. I thought Oughter Brigg was a good, honest dog and I was happy to have him. I remember getting the dog from him at the Irish Cup in Clounanna. I was a bit taken aback by his size. He was as big as a bull — but I remember thinking: 'At least he's been well-fed.' It

Josie McKenna receives the trophy from Minister for Agriculture Mark Clinton after Ballybeg Prim had been voted 1975 Greyhound of the Year.

The great bitch Nameless Pixie, twice a finalist in the Irish Derby.

took us a long time to get his weight right. But he ran very genuinely after that. The semi-final of the Irish Derby was the only really bad race I remember him running while he was with me."

By then, Oughter Brigg had become Ger McKenna's fourth winner of the Irish Cesarewitch. Low Sail, which had been so close in that Guinness 600 decider, was running as well as ever but Easy Silver, owned by Liam Brady and trained by Matt Travers, went off the odds-on favourite. It looked all over at halfway with Easy Silver stretching out in front. But Oughter Brigg began to close and, showing acceleration not typical of a staying type, he out-paced the market leader and won, going away. Remarkably, having run 33.48, 33.42 and 33.46 in the preliminaries, McKenna had conjured up a time of 33.08, one of the fastest ever over Navan's 600 yards, from the three-year-old. A measure of the achievement is that Easy Silver went to the final of the Irish Cesarewitch the next year when it took Keystone Prince, again trained by Travers for Brady, to beat him.

The main attraction about Butterfly Billy was that he was by Pigalle Wonder.

"He was owned by a Corkman call O'Riordan, if I'm not mistaken," says Ger. "I took the dog after he had run a couple of races at Cork. It was the same as Yanka Boy. I had stayed back to see him race simply because he was by Clonalvy Pride and that's how we bought him. Butterfly Billy was an honest-to-goodness dog, perfectly suited to 600 yards. He won the Midland Cesarewitch at Mullingar and still holds the record for the trip there. Then he won the Irish Cesarewitch and he was beaten in a photo-finish for the Longford Derby."

Butterfly Billy was McKenna's first Cesarewitch winner and in the 1965 decider he recorded an exceptionally fast time of 33.26. When the Borrisokane trainer repeated classic success in this event with Yanka Boy (33.38) in 1967 and Ballybeg Prim (33.30) in 1975, neither dog could match Butterfly Billy's time. Ballypeg Prim, in his Irish Cesarewitch year, won the Guinness 600 and came back again in 1976 to complete a double in the Shelbourne Park feature, which is regarded as just about the most prestigious non-classic on the calendar. Itsachampion had previously won it in 1972. McKenna rates the 600 yards at Shelbourne Park, where the run-up is the length of the home straight, as one of the supreme and most ideal tests for a greyhound. But he seldom contests the early-season Guinness 600 these days, especially if he thinks a greyhound is destined for bigger things in the middle distance sphere.

"It's at the wrong time now, as far as I'm concerned," he says. "It used to be held after the Irish Derby and that made more sense. The fact is, you build a dog up with regards to distance. You run him over 525 yards and then progress to 600 yards — not the other way around. Own Pride was caught on the line by Itsamint in the 1969 Guinness 600, that was after he had won the Derby. He certainly would not have contested the event if the Irish Derby was still to come."

Here's Tat (Here Sonny — Spiral Dash) won the Guinness 600 in 1977, but that was before McKenna trained the Alfie McLean-owned dog. Under McKenna, Here's Tat ran up the following year's Irish Derby; but McKenna never fancied him. "He was a soft old dog," he recalls.

As well as sponsoring the Irish Derby, P.J. Carroll and Co., the cigarette firm based in Dundalk, had also begun supporting the International 525 at their local track. It was to be the richest single greyhound race in Britain and Ireland. Dundalk promoted it well, and energetically sought the top three British-trained greyhounds and the season's outstanding trio on the home front. The list of winners illustrates just how successful Dundalk was in their objective. Seldom has a year gone by since 1968, when McKenna has not had a representative. Time Up Please (29.60) and Bashful Man (29.70) won in 1972 and 1973 respectively, and Nameless Pixie performed her usual heroics when getting up to win in 1979. The bitch, which gave McKenna his only Irish Oaks success when she scored in 1979, was highly rated by the trainer.

"She was perhaps the most honest greyhound we ever trained. She got knocked down in races and still got up and won."

Rugged Mick ran the opposition into the ground in 29.34 in 1984. But McKenna claims an almost total disinterest in track records.

"What time they do makes absolutely no difference. If they do 32 seconds; it doesn't matter as long as they win."

Dundalk now slots well into the trainer's plans, coming between the English Derby and its Irish equivalent. If nothing else, it is a pipe-opener before the premier classic at Shelbourne Park.

Move Gas (1969) and Tantallon's Flyer (1975) both won the Easter Cup over 525 yards for McKenna, but this traditional curtain-raiser on the season proper at Shelbourne Park has never held much of an attraction for the handler: "It's very early and my dogs are simply not ready," he says. The Albert Lucas owned Always Keen (Always Proud — Liber Latinus) rated by McKenna as "a middling sort of dog, not really top class", won the Irish Puppy Derby at Harold's Cross in 1968. The same success went to Joe O'Connor's Shamrock Point (Monalee Champion — Gruelling Point) in 1974, and Hammond (Tranquility Sea — Run For Cover), owned by Gerry O'Connor, Tullamore, Co. Offaly, in 1977. But even if these dogs never went on to achieve much afterwards, McKenna's trio in the 1979 Puppy Derby gave him one of his most memorable nights.

Mick O'Toole swapped the leash for the reins and succeeded famously at training horses where he had failed with greyhounds. He took out a trainer's licence with the Turf Club in 1966 and won the Cheltenham Gold Cup with Davy Lad in 1977; and the 1979 Irish 2,000 Guineas with Dickins Hill. This horse was also second in both the Epsom Derby and Irish Derby in the same year. Evidently O'Toole must have felt lucky in 1979, for when McKenna suggested that he should buy a greyhound belonging to Ned Kennedy of Cashel, Co. Tipperary, he did not hesitate and Tivoli Cant was purchased. The dog went to the Puppy Derby final, so did his kennel companions: Ballyard Pine owned by Michael Daly and Silent Prince owned by Billy Mann.

"Mick O'Toole had flown in from Ascot with Kevin Prendergast for the race and I remember Kevin saying something to the effect that Micko's dog had better win, after all the trouble they had gone to," recalls McKenna.

They would never know just how lucky they were . . . Ballyard Pine had been coughing throughout the competition, but suddenly appeared to be shaking off its effects and finding his form again. But when he finished the final, he was found to have lost part of his tail. It had caught in the trap door. On the same night as Tivoli Cant and Ballyard Pine were qualifying, the electricity failed at Harold's Cross and Silent Prince had to run his semi-final on the following Tuesday, three days before the decider. The only one to avoid any mishap was Tivoli Cant (Can't Decide — Swanky Debbie). On the night, Tivoli Cant came from behind Silent Prince (Supreme Fun — Pop Corn), with Ballyard Pine (Rita's Choice — Pineapple Grand) flying at the finish. The three flashed across the line together, with Tivoli Cant a head in front of

Silent Prince and Ballyard Pine only three parts of a length further back.

Tony Brennan's Lauragh Six (Garradrimna — Emmerdale Pride) was another McKenna runner to win the Puppy Derby. He clocked 29.04, which was the fastest time since the feature switched to 525 yards in 1951. At that stage in 1983, he had already annexed the Shelbourne Park sprint track record of 19.33. After the Puppy Derby he came back to face Kenny Linzell's English challenger Upton Rocket and Pa Fitzgerald's Seventh Wonder over two bends at Ringsend. Lauragh Six made it a procession in 19.39. But he could also stay 525 yards, as he showed on Irish Laurels night, which was held late in September that year. It was quite an evening for McKenna, who decided to run four dogs and placed a £200 four-dog accumulator with the bookmakers. All four won: Tony Brennan's Brideview Sailor in 16.64 and Lauragh Six in 28.96; Eamonn McLoughney's Back Garden won the Laurels in 29.66 and Cathal McCarthy's Count Five scored in 29.09.

"Lauragh Six was quite a dog," says McKenna. "If he was still running, he would be doing 19.15 or even 19.10 at Shelbourne Park."

The Tipperary Cup at Thurles was claimed by the McKenna kennel in 1980 by Carrick Chance, owned by the Athlone, Co. Westmeath, butcher Sean Dunning, again in 1982 when Patsy Byrne's Shinrone Jet scored in 29.20. But Ger has a particular regret about the 1986 Tipperary Cup, when Master Mystery (Ballyheigue Moon — Susie's Liberator), which would go on to win the £4,500 Respond Champion Stakes at Shelbourne Park, just failed by a short head. The occasion left a void in a career, in which most would imagine that all ambitions had been fulfilled.

Ger recalls: "It had always been my ambition to meet Lester Piggott. He was always my great hero — and no matter what he did or what they say about him, he still is. Anyway, one Wednesday night I noticed Lester was riding at the Phoenix Park and I decided that, instead of going to the dogs, I would go up to Dublin to try and meet Lester. 'Twinny' Byrne was with me and he decided that we would position ourselves at the exit from the winner's enclosure. So, out comes Lester and over goes 'Twinny' and grabs him by the arm and tells him to come and meet 'the great Ger McKenna.' Poor old Lester didn't know what was happening, and I doubt if he knew who I was. But he came over and shook hands as 'Twinny' reeled off all the winners I'd trained."

Lauragh Six: Winner 1983 Puppy Derby.

A measure of one maestro's admiration for the other was that when Follow A Star went across the line, as perhaps the least great of the trainer's Irish Laurels winners in 1985, McKenna would remember it as the night that he surpassed Piggott's classic tally of twenty-eight winners. The following year, Piggott was bowing out and included in his itinerary an unusual public appearance. Showing the kind of initiative so often lacking in the presentation of the sport in Ireland, Thurles had arranged for the jockey to hand over the trophy for that season's Tipperary Cup.

"I never wanted a dog to win so much," says Ger. "If Master Myles had won, I would have shaken Lester Piggott's hand again."

After a protracted photo-finish, Master Myles was deemed the loser by the minimum margin.

CHAPTER NINE

The Irish Laurels

C HANGING times and changing dates have seen Ger McKenna alter the emphasis which he puts on certain events. The Guinness 600 is too long in distance for greyhounds running early in the season; the Easter Cup is too early so that his greyhounds are not really ready. When Back Garden won the Irish Laurels in 1983, the classic was in September. When he returned to Cork to challenge in the final, won by kennel companion Rugged Mick, the following season it was in the month of July that he went. True, McKenna completed the Irish Laurels hat-trick in 1985; but an equal truth is that this was the extent of the ambitions for the winner Follow A Star. McKenna has not travelled north of the Border for some time to contest the Guinness-sponsored Irish National Sprint at Dunmore Stadium in Belfast, where the Bramwich hare is now in use. His last winner, of what is an August classic, was Move Gas in 1969. It was 1976 when he won the National Breeders Two-Year-Old Produce Stakes with Cill Dubh Darkey at Clonmel. Not everyone has appreciated the changes to sand and Bramwich hare at the Co. Tipperary venue, but its late April running is perhaps not an incentive to a trainer with designs on the English Derby. Oughter Brigg was an extended distance dog and it was expected that the Irish Cesarewitch at Navan in 1987 would be his main objective. The Irish Cesarewitch is a July classic at which McKenna is seldom seen. The Irish Oaks, which McKenna won for the one and only time in 1979 with Nameless Pixie, is a June classic. He hardly ever contests the bitch classic any more, and he has never bothered with the Irish Grand National through the years.

The Irish classic calendar reads: Late-April: Produce Stakes (confined to pups); early-June: Irish Oaks (confined to bitches); late-June: English Derby; early-July: Irish Cesarewitch; mid-July: Irish Laurels; mid-August: Irish National Sprint; mid-September: Irish Derby; late-October: Irish St Leger.

McKenna has won all of these and — with the exception of the Oaks — he has taken them on more than one occasion. But the table has two confined classics, the Produce Stakes and Oaks, and two major middle-distance classics in the Laurels and Cesarewitch, with the English Derby, which takes the top greyhounds and top trainers like Ger McKenna out of the scene for six weeks, sandwiched in-between. For a trainer of McKenna's calibre, who advocates freshness in a dog as a primary dictum, the result is that the Clonmel, Harold's Cross, Navan and Cork classics — half of those on the Irish classic list — have to suffer. They will not have McKenna involved and he, as all realise, is a huge drawing card. McKenna can be a stubborn man — *is* a stubborn man — and one can only see the authorities having to change their dates before he changes his ways. The English Derby, Dundalk International, Irish Derby and Irish St Leger — a lifetime in greyhound racing has taught Ger McKenna that these are the most important objectives. Perhaps even more fundamentally, he has learnt that to win all of these, it is essential that, barring a couple of preparation races early in the term, a good greyhound should not be run anywhere else. A dog is just not able to sustain the effort all-year-round. McKenna would bluntly prefer to succeed in the Big Four than fail by contesting every classic in the book.

But there were nights, glorious nights, at Cork, the picturesque track squeezed between the University and the Western Road. The night that Eamonn McLoughney's Back Garden was the winner of the 1983 Irish Laurels, initiating a classic treble which the great McKenna had achieved in the previous decade with Ballybeg Prim, Nameless Star and Red Rasper in the Irish St Leger. McKenna made a slow start in the Cork classic and his Laurels breakthrough came in 1970 with Gabriel Boy, owned by Pat Dalton, belatedly compensating him for Prince of Bermuda running up the classic in 1956.

McKenna does not enthuse about his first Laurels success: "Gabriel Boy was a good starter. But he was probably lucky enough to draw trap six, where he wanted to be, in four rounds."

English Derby finalist Ballymaclune ran up the Cork classic in 1974

Pat Dalton, now America's leading trainer and then owner of the Ger McKenna-trained Gabriel Boy after the dog's success in the 1970 Irish Laurels in Cork.

Back Garden, winner of the 1983 Laurels.   *N and B Photos*

and then Nameless Star (Rita's Choice — Itsastar), which had been the middle part of the McKenna Irish St Leger hat-trick (1975–77), became the trainer's second Irish Laurels winner in 1976. Nameless Star ran in the name of Mrs Rita McAuley, whose husband Ben, a Belfast contract cleaner, was unusual in that he patronised the kennels of both McKenna cousins, Ger and Gay. His Irish Cesarewitch winner Rita's Choice — sire to Nameless Star — had been with the Cabinteely handler.

"McAuley bought Nameless Star's dam from Leslie NcNair, as I remember it," says Ger. "He was quite a lucky owner and had all the Nameless dogs. He was not a universally popular man, but I always got on very well with him. I could not fault him."

Nameless Star had his most promising early showing when winning in 29.15 at Kilkenny, and then he ran behind his kennel companion Right Moordyke, winner of the Midland Puppy Stake at Mullingar. He joined Yanka Boy (St Leger–Cesarewitch), Ballybeg Prim (St Leger–Cesarewitch) and Own Pride (Derby–St Leger) in a quartet of McKenna dogs which have won two different classics, when he won the Laurels in 29.30. He was a greyhound with bad kidneys and taxed McKenna's patience more than most.

The Borrisokane trainer had to wait until 1979 for his third Laurels victory, when he fielded Knockrour Slave (Sole Aim — Knockrour Exile). Denis Lynch had won the Cork classic with Knockrour Girl the previous year and had started Knockrour Slave off with a win in the 1979 Guinness Trophy, during which he recorded a time of 29.05. He again showed his liking for the Leeside track when taking the Laurels in 29.45.

"The owner just rang me up and asked me to take Knockrour Slave. He was a shockin' well bred dog," says Ger.

His main objective for the following year was the English Derby — but from the start, things did not go well. McKenna felt that Knockrour Slave needed the outside but official prompting at White City saw him drawn inside Atlantic Expert, which the connections fancied and had backed at 150-1, in an English Derby trial. Knockrour Slave shifted wide; Atlantic Expert was injured and out of the Blue Riband. Knockrour Slave beat Indian Joe, the eventual winner, along with Nameless Pixie in the Derby proper, but was eliminated when a leading fancy in the semi-finals. McKenna's faith in Knockrour Slave was undimmed and he brought him back to Cork where he drew trap six in the final and ran the 525 yards in 29 seconds to give owner Denis Lynch an Irish Laurels hat-trick. Perhaps the most accurate measure of Knockrour Slave's achievement in the 1980 final was that his time of 29.00 for 525 yards was equal to that recorded by Rather Grand when he beat Prince of Bermuda in 1956. The difference was that Rather Grand's Laurels was run over 500 yards.

Back Garden's victory run in the 1983 Laurels marked the start of McKenna's three-year domination of the classic. It was an unforgettable night when Back Garden was the third leg of a McKenna four-timer, completed by Brideview Sailor, Lauragh Six and Count Five. A night when the word infallible did not seem sacrilegious. The following year McKenna went into the final mob-handed. They went to traps: North Yard (Sandman — Pula), owned by Cathal McCarthy and trained by Ger McKenna; Back Garden (Knockrour Slave — Sweeping Bally), owned by Eamonn McLoughney and trained by Ger McKenna; Diamond Boy (Parkdown Jet — Diamond Ace), owned by Denis Diffley and trained by Matt O'Donnell; Manorville Sand (Sandman — Westmead City), owned and trained by Mrs Catherine Doran; Rugged Mick (Ceili Band — Blueberry Pet) owned by Pat Murphy and trained by Ger McKenna; Coolmona Man (Killaclug Jet — Knockrour Minnie) owned and trained by Denis Lynch.

In respects other than name, it was a classic final. O'Donnell from Killenaule, Co. Tipperary, had four track classics at this point in his career and would soon double that tally. The Dorans from Thurles, Co. Tipperary, were in the process of building a racing and breeding dynasty on a par with any in the country. Denis Lynch, Aghabulloge, Co. Cork, was seeking his fourth Irish Laurels with the dog which had started favourite, but had been unplaced to Back Garden the previous year. They bet: 5-4 Rugged Mick, 9-4 Back Garden, 4-1 Manorville Sand, 6-1 Coolmona Man, North Yard, 28-1 Diamond Boy. Rugged Mick, bred by Ger McKenna the younger, slayed the field with his awesome early pace and held a clear advantage as they turned down the back straight. Back Garden was tucked behind in second place and trying to close. A chorus of appreciation went up. It was not provoked by Rugged Mick's pace, nor Back Garden's stamina. North Yard had moved into third place. McKenna was going to sweep the boards. The final details told it all. Manorville Sand, beaten a total of over nine lengths, was the nearest in fourth to any of the McKenna dogs. The next year the unstoppable McKenna completed his hat-trick with Follow A Star (Under Par — Float A Loan). The winning time was 29.42.

McKenna is always totally honest in his assessment of dogs and his verdict can sometimes surprise. A personal observation is that the 1983 Laurels winner, Back Garden, represents genuineness, the quality above all else — pace, stamina or any other attribute — that McKenna rates most highly in a greyhound.

McKenna says: "Yes, he turned out very genuine, but he was very soft at the start. Sean McLoughney brought him here, he was qualified and then he won a race in Galway in 18.70. Then we put him away for the winter. In his first full season he won in 29.70 at Shelbourne Park and we ran him in Cork. But we were disappointed with the way he performed in the Produce Stakes at Clonmel. He first started to show what he was made of when he started running in the Laurels which he won. The third year, he went to England and qualified for the consolation in the English Derby and then went to the Laurels final again. The race I remember him best for was the 1983 Anglo-Irish International, when he ran a blinder. Without a doubt, he was a dog that was running at his best the nearer he came to the end of his career."

That International night in 1983 saw a typical swashbuckling display from the McKenna dogs. Richard Liffey's Run To Score (Time Up Please — Fiona's Move) won in 32.14 for 575 yards, Lauragh Six was equal to the international sprint challenge against Upton Rocket and Seventh Wonder in 19.39 and Back Garden won the Guinness-sponsored £3,000 Anglo-Irish in 29.37.

It was only the fact that Mrs Elizabeth Furlong's Ramtogue Champ (Witches Champion — Rushin Out) ran up the £2,000 Shelbourne Leger final, that failed to make it another McKenna clean-sweep. It was not the first time that McKenna had come to the rescue of Bord Na gCon — and national pride — in the Anglo-Irish International which had been revived at the start of the decade. Run on a strictly British-bred versus Irish-bred format, the British took the competition by storm with a 1981 double for Gigolo Diomides. Further embarrassment was inflicted in the following season by Duke Of Hazard and his colleagues. McKenna, who did not take part in the preceding years, got into the action in 1983 and the home reputation

Owen with his father's 1976 winner of the Guinness Trophy at Cork, Mountleader Omar.

was restored to some extent when Back Garden out-paced the London winner Glatton Grange. The representative competition was to prove most informative to McKenna in the following campaign when Rugged Mick became his first runner at Wimbledon since it had just been announced that it was to replace the defunct White City as the home of the Greyhound Derby. Rugged Mick failed at Wimbledon but in a return leg at Shelbourne Park, which represented greyhound racing at its very best, Moran's Beef overtook Rugged Mick at the third bend and led a McKenna one-two.

If Back Garden, in the end, could be classed as among the most honest or determined of the McKenna runners, then Rugged Mick must surely rate as one of his top exponents of front running. He was bought from Michael Brunnock for Belfast painting and decorating contractor Pat Murphy. McKenna gave him the winter off and re-introduced him at Tralee. Murphy, a fearless punter, arrived by air in the Co. Kerry capital, which at that time had a handkerchief of an air strip at Farranfore, and wiped the bookmakers' boards clean. Rugged Mick was out and running when the opposition was trying to get into its stride. Away and gone. It would be the same in the Laurels and in the Carrolls International at Dundalk.

McKenna comments: "I cannot rightly think of what would lead him to the first bend. There weren't too many. Thinking back, I feel that we could have given him a run around Shelbourne Park before the Irish Derby. He wasn't around Ringsend for a long time and he totally mistimed his break when he went out early."

Greyhound racing is unusual — off-hand I would say it is unique — in that it makes no allowance for sex. Bitches compete on equal terms with dogs and I know of no equivalent situation in sport. Horse racing sees fillies get an allowance in weight, and even the rules of coursing dictate that bitches should be guarded in all-age competition. It stands to reason that for a bitch to compete on the same level with male opposition — and win — then she must be exceptional. There have been a handful of great racing bitches; and females have won both the Irish and English Derby. Nameless Pixie (Monalee Champion — Itsastar) did not win a Derby, but she contested two finals of the Irish version when the distance of 525 yards was short of her best.

"If the Irish Derby had been over today's classic distance of 550 yards, she would probably have won," says McKenna. "I got her at a

Ger with Proud Choice after her win in the Barry Cup at Navan. Owner A.S. Lucas receives the trophy from Paddy O'Neill (right), then a sports commentator and later Chairman of Bord na gCon.

very early stage and she was a great bitch. Without doubt 550 yards was her job.

"She was desperately unlucky not to win the Irish St Leger but showed in the Oaks and in the Dundalk International that she was an exceptional greyhound."

McKenna's bitch dominated the 1979 campaign when she took the Dundalk International in 29.82 and triumphed at Harold's Cross with an Oaks victory in 29.34. McKenna is more dismissive of his two winners of the National Breeders Produce Stakes. Kilkennyman Tom Duggan's Big Kuda won in 1973 and is remembered as "a surly sort of dog" and Cill Dubh Darkey, owned by Michael Bergin, Freshford, Co. Kilkenny, took honours in 1976. But McKenna's brace of Irish National Sprint winners left more of an impression. The competition over 435 yards is perfect for coursing-bred dogs, with Dunmore

Ger with Proud Jane, winner of the Barry Cup at Navan.

Stadium's huge dimensions — in Irish terms — and its long, galloping, straights. The Pat Dalton-owned Bauhus set the ball rolling in 1965 with a win in 23.73. The Richard Liffey-owned Move Gas, winner in 1969 was beaten a final to the Cork Cup and also ran up the all-aged at Lixnaw in Co. Kerry. He went on to win the Easter Cup at Shelbourne Park in the same year but he trialled badly at Harold's Cross and, perhaps, had had enough of track racing at that stage.

CHAPTER TEN

The Racing Kennel

THERE are professional greyhound trainers, and there are those who are professional at training greyhounds. They are not one and the same thing, and yet Ger McKenna is both. He is in a different league to many of those holding licences. He would not put it that way himself. Perhaps he would not want it put that way, but the past results say it is so and the everyday results still say it is so. McKenna has the advantage of having watched and listened to his father; of growing up in a greyhound town and county. He has the advantage of experience, which only age can bring and which no book-learning can instil; and of having three able sons who will watch and listen in the place where he spent his childhood. They share his devotion, his attention to detail. Keeping a greyhound in training with Ger McKenna is not an expensive business — £25 per week — but no money can buy the care with which your greyhound is treated. McKenna's way of life is a vocation as much as a profession. The kennel strength is never big, thirty-five at most, and every dog — with all its good and bad points — is known individually. Sometimes they have pet names, but more often they are known by the owner's name or simply their colour.

"Take the black fella out. Leave the brindled fella . . ." They are the most common colours on the greyhound chart; yet John, Ger and Owen know instantly to which one The Boss is referring. And he is the boss when there is work to be done, no doubt about that. The public see him in various guises: the Irish ambassador for the sport when he is at the English Derby; the most successful trainer in the game; the public relations officer for the family firm when the media ring; father and husband when the photograph is taken after a big win; a consoling voice to the owner whose dog did not win; the hard-headed businessman when a good dog surfaces in any corner of the country. But here and now, he is the employer.

It is mealtime for the dogs; the main meal. The chef is cunning. Earlier, just after noon, the dogs have been given a liquid with a pink hue. It must taste as bad as it looks.

"It cleans them out," said Ger. "But they won't drink it by itself, you have to throw in a little mince, just a pinch, to make it more palatable. It will also sharpen up their appetites." They wait until after the family lunch, and then it's back to the kennel kitchen. Here Ger McKenna, all things to all dogs, trainer, master, companion — turns alchemist. You have to watch carefully as he does it, it's like the three-card trick. But there are nine containers and he uses multiple combinations and variations as he conjures with the feed bowls, which are spanking clean and filled to the brim with prime meat.

The contents include: calcium powder, seaweed in powder form, cider vinegar, red liquid in an unmarked bottle, unidentified tablets in a jar, an unlabelled fluid, Sanatogen tablets, Rubex tablets and Vitamin E tablets.

What are they all for? There's the rub: "Ah, they all do something for them," says Ger. You are conscious of intruding on something private, a master mystery. They help with strengthening bones, with burning off fatty tissues, with cleansing, with weight, with cramp, with nerves . . . These are *his* secrets. Nothing is left to chance, nothing is neglected. So much can go wrong and prevention is less trouble than cure. McKenna does not give much away, but he is prepared to outline his basic strategy.

COUGH: "The best prevention against a whole kennel getting the cough is to inject all newcomers. If you put a few cut onions into the kennels, that kills a lot of what is in the atmosphere. Some dogs will be immune to it, even if a number in the kennel have the cough. If you are in any doubt, don't run the dog. The virus spreads easily, going from one place to another. But I've found that isolating dogs does not make a great deal of difference. I would avoid running an affected greyhound for a week to ten days. The less you put the dog through at this stage, the better they will recover. "It's just like yourself. If you are feeling out of sorts, the best cure is to stay in bed for two or three days. So just let the dog rest up."

DIARRHOEA: "Give the dog two Strinacin tablets and no food. You can possibly let it have a slice of white loaf, but otherwise, cut out the grub."

NAILS: "Cut and file the nails regularly."

TEETH: "We give the dogs big bones to chew on and that is good for their teeth, but we vomit them regularly as they might be at a bone for up to two hours."

NERVOUS: "There is no use telling you a lie, but one way out is to give a dog a couple of bitches. I am not too fond of nervous dogs. Now, Itsachampion was definitely a head-case. There is not a lot you can do for a dog like that. Try to get to know the dog so it will trust you. I was the first to get to know Itsachampion and he responded to me, so I always paraded him myself. But a really nervous dog can upset a whole kennel, and you're just as well to get rid of it."

TOES: "There are apparently a couple of new methods for treating toe injuries, but I still prefer to have them pin-fired."

TICKS: "We have never had a problem with ticks or fleas. If we did, I would just clean out the kennel and spray with DDT and Jeyes Fluid."

WORMS: "Our dogs are wormed straightaway when they get here, and then every month."

TRACK LEG: "Vaseline is the job there, so that the legs do not make a hard contact."

Even after all that attention, your dog may not turn out a winner, a classic winner, at any rate. It is very hard to come up with an exact percentage but Josie guesses that about one in ten will not make the grade.

"We don't keep them too long if we feel that they are not going to make it," she says. "A month or six weeks is usually long enough to make an assessment. Most of the owners want it that way. They like to be told straight out if the dog is not good enough. They trust us to tell them the truth." She reckons that they have been lucky with owners.

"The bigger the gambler, the bigger the headache," Ger interjects. "Of course, we have had the odd owner who felt that his dog hadn't been done right. I remember one the year that we had three dogs in a race. One was Butterfly Billy which won. But we fancied another one in the race and one of the beaten owners was none too pleased. In that situation we would like the three dogs to go across the line together, but it just doesn't happen that way.

"We *have* been lucky with our owners. We charge £25 and we do not charge for trials and other extras, but it can still be expensive. Take the English Derby. That lasts for six to seven weeks and there's transport, kennels, various fees, accommodation, petrol — all things like that, to be taken into account. It adds up to at least £2,000 and that has nothing to do with the price of the dog, the size of the owner's bet and the cost of going over to England to see the dog run."

In the old days it was different. Now there is pressure on McKenna, pressure to come up with the goods. Owners used to ring up, like the time when Tom O'Doherty offered him Own Pride. Now the reverse is the case. An owner rings McKenna, and he does not have a dog. He wants McKenna to find him one.

"I like a bit of breeding," says Ger. "I like to know that the sire is throwing good dogs. Some are not throwing good dogs consistently and the result is that we end up with all shapes and sizes. I don't like a dog that is too big. Lartigue Note was plenty big enough. I think seventy to seventy-five pounds is about right. I believe that the weight of dogs has got out of hand. Mad Tanist and Marsh Harrier, two great dogs, weighed sixty one pounds and Move Handy, which was a coursing dog, was only seventy-one pounds. I also hate wall-eyed dogs, the dogs which have a fixed stare. It is probably nothing more than a superstition but I like to avoid dogs with cocked-up ears. I don't like to see an undershot mouth but Crafty Killer, a very good dog we had early on for Martin Divilly, was undershot and it never really affected him. Generally I like to see a dog with a tidy back, straight hindlegs and a narrow chest."

When Mckenna has found his dog and is confident that it is sound, settled in and trained to fitness, he decides where to run it. This is important, all-important. It is an art; and McKenna is its master. It is the one thing that is pure instinct, even more than being able to look at a dog and accurately predict the weight at which it should race. McKenna got it wrong once — with Rathgallen Tady. But that was the singular exception. He knows every track inside out and is uncompromising in his opinion.

CLONMEL: "It's a good track and its sand surface is terrific. I am not too gone on the Bramwich hare, but for safety it could not be beaten." *Classic wins: Produce Stakes (2).*

CORK: "This is a very well-run track, these days. I would always like

to be drawn in trap six here. But, given a choice, I would like to run from trap six at every track." *Classic wins: Irish Laurels (6)*.

DUNDALK: "Extremely tight, it's essential that you have a good starter."

DUNMORE: " A great galloping track for big galloping dogs but it is an awful long way to go. We used to set out in the morning to get there in time for the trials which were at 8 pm." *Classic wins: Irish National Sprint (2)*.

ENNISCORTHY: "I have not raced here since I got married. I have nothing against it; but it's an awkward hundred-mile journey."

GALWAY: "This has been a lucky old track for me. It's got the reputation of being slow, but a good dog should be still capable of running 29.40 there."

HAROLD'S CROSS: "It's just all right. I'm not gone on it." *Classic wins: Irish Oaks (1)*.

KILKENNY: "This is a great favourite of mine, although a dog needs to come out quickly. It looks a narrow track, but a pacey dog runs very well here. I like the way the bends are banked."

LIFFORD: "It's a credit to the management. In all my years I do not think I have ever been more impressed with any place. It would be worth the while of all other track managers to drive up and have a look at the place. Of course, it is a long, long, journey for us. If it was nearer, I would be there every night. The kennels are first-class. The cleanliness of the whole track is what struck me and when I went up recently and there was an adequate place to wash the dogs' feet after racing. I took Lartigue Note and Lodge Dancer there and they both came very well out of the races."

LIMERICK: "I've got a lot of good memories of the place, apart from the fact that it was the first track I ever visited. A peculiarity is that all greyhounds seem to come up the centre of the track. I have never had a dog — and some of them were definite railers — which would come up the wire. I don't know why that should be, because the number one trap is out a bit and gives the dog plenty of room on the inside. I would love to know how Lartigue Note would have negotiated it. But even he, I imagine, would have come off the rail. Another point about the Market's Field is that the finishing line is on the first bend. Dogs tend to be easing off, as if taking the corner, at the finish." *Classic wins: Irish St Leger (12)*.

LONGFORD: "A good galloping track, but it is not the most convenient place for owners to get to."

MULLINGAR: "I find it a hard, tough track. I used to go there very often, but you can't go everywhere."

NAVAN: "I am not very fond of it these days, for the simple reason that it lacks atmosphere." *Classic wins: Irish Cesarewitch (4).*

NEWBRIDGE: "It's just all right. It's exceptionally fast, and you need a good starter."

SHELBOURNE PARK: "As a race track, it is quite simply the best. It always has been." *Classic wins: Irish Derby (3).*

THURLES: "You want a good, galloping dog here. There's a great sprint, but that third bend — the County Home bend — will always find out a weak one."

TRALEE: "It's probably exceptional among Irish tracks in that you need an inside draw in a 525 or 550. It's a good test. Your dog wants to be able to start *and* stay. It has a tricky uphill back straight and downhill run home."

WATERFORD: "I don't get there as often as I would like. It's a fair track and has a good atmosphere."

YOUGHAL: "A very well-kept track. It is sandy and safe."

CHAPTER ELEVEN

A–Z of Practical Hints

BY coincidence, Ger McKenna has trained a classic winner for almost every year in which he has been a greyhound trainer. He took out his original licence in 1956 and in thirty-three years his classic total had reached thirty-two. That is where the coincidence ends. The facts show that in the three full decades in which he has operated, McKenna has maintained a remarkable evenness. Leaving out Prince of Bermuda in the fifties, McKenna trained ten classic winners in the Sixties, twelve in the Seventies and added another nine by the close of the Eighties. At the age of fifty-nine, he was far from finished. A message he hammered out with Lartigue Note's pulsating English Derby win at Wimbledon in 1989. Indeed, in one respect, McKenna has been turning out more individual winners in the last nine years. He sent out nine individual classic winners in the Eighties, while two dogs — Yanka Boy and Own Pride — gave him four classics in the Sixties; and three dogs — Time Up Please, Ballybeg Prim and Nameless Star — contributed six classics to his quota in the Seventies. There have been twenty-two other dogs which have won a single classic.

McKenna's Classic Progress

1956 — Prince of Bermuda (St Leger): 1.
1960 — Swanlands Best (St Leger): 1.
1962 — Apollo Again (St Leger): 1.
1965 — Lovely Chieftain (St Leger); Butterfly Billy (Cesarewitch); Bauhus (National Sprint): 3.
1967 — Yanka Boy (St Leger); Yanka Boy (Cesarewitch): 2.
1969 — Own Pride (Irish Derby); Own Pride (St Leger); Move Gas (National Sprint): 3.

1970 — Gabriel Boy (Laurels): 1.
1971 — Time Up Please (St Leger): 1.
1972 — Time Up Please (St Leger): 1.
1973 — Bashful Man (Irish Derby); Big Kuda (Produce Stakes): 2.
1975 — Ballybeg Prim (St Leger); Ballybeg Prim (Cesarewitch): 2.
1976 — Nameless Star (St Leger); Nameless Star (Laurels); Cill Dubh Darkey (Produce): 3.
1977 — Red Rasper (St Leger): 1.
1979 — Nameless Pixie (Oaks): 1.
1980 — Knockrour Slave (Laurels): 1.
1981 — Parkdown Jet (English Derby): 1.
1983 — Back Garden (Laurels): 1.
1984 — Moran's Beef (St Leger); Rugged Mick (Laurels): 2.
1985 — Follow A Star (Laurels): 1.
1987 — Rathgallen Tady (Irish Derby); Oughter Brigg (Cesarewitch): 2.
1989 — Lartigue Note (English Derby): 1.

There is no element of fluke in the record. It could be argued that if anything, McKenna gets better at his trade. The only reason that his charges in this decade have not been double-classic winners is perhaps that the handler has tended to be more sparing with them. He is a man who has learnt from the mistakes of others — and his own. He can talk with authority and experience on every aspect of the greyhound; how it functions or malfunctions; how it responds to those around it or, conversely, why it fails to respond. Here, for the first time, he reveals the secrets of his training methods in a series of practical hints.

AGE: "I don't like to see dogs raced too early, sixteen to eighteen months is plenty soon enough. Bitches, as they tend to be more developed, can race as young as fourteen or fifteen months. That was one of the things that attracted me to Lartigue Note. He was only fourteen months when I spotted him. That was too young in my book but, at the same time, I felt that because he was so young he might improve a lot. In my opinion, dogs are at their peak when they have just turned two years of age. I like going into a Derby final with a dog around that age. They are still fresh. Trainers in England tend to over-run them early. I got a dog, Angelo Carlotti, over from England and I was staggered at the amount of form he had. It literally ran into pages.

"If the dog looks like he might make it at stud, then I would be putting him away at three-years-old. I have found that dogs run too much will not be as good as expected at stud. The racing probably affects their hearts and many of their pups turn out to be useless. Champion Prince was a great stud dog. He had to be retired after an accident when he burnt his back. But I believe that he wouldn't have been as great as a sire if he had been kept in training and if the accident hadn't forced him to go to stud when he did."

BITCHES: "We have never kept too many bitches. There was Nameless Pixie, of course, and we had Sweeping Bally and Sweeping Maid. Basically, I prefer to travel bitches separately from dogs and put them in different paddocks; and that is not always practical. But that said, when a bitch is right, she is easier to keep right. We kept hold of Sweeping Bally, which was by Sand Man and threw Back Garden, simply because she belonged to young Ger and he was devoted to her. He was only thirteen or fourteen when he was offered £3,000 for her. But he wouldn't sell. He was heartbroken when she died. She's buried out there in the paddocks."

COLOUR: "I have a thing about blue dogs. I don't know what it is exactly, but if there were ten pups in a litter, the last one I would pick would be the blue one. In fact, it was the one thing that put me off Parkdown Jet. His colour and his breeding. But it was the colour that blocked me a small bit. It's just something about the blue. After all, you don't see too many of them around. Of course, Parkdown Jet turned out to be one of the best dogs I ever had."

DISTANCES: "The 360 yards at Shelbourne Park is my personal favourite in terms of race distances. I love the sprint races there. One race over 360 at Ringsend is worth ten trials in my book. At the other end of the scale, I have never been keen on marathon racing, although we did have greyhounds like Proud Molly which won the Corn Cuchulainn at Harold's Cross in 1967. But I wouldn't be pushed about even looking at a marathon or a hurdle race. At the same time, I accept that they are crowdpullers."

EARS AND EYES: "Draughts are the main cause of eye problems. If a dog happens to get sore eyes, we just wash them with a little bit of cotton-wool and cold tea. The ears are cleaned regularly with cotton-wool and a dab of methylated spirits. We have never had too many problems with eyes and ears. The biggest problem you will ever have with a dog is if you find he has no heart. Give me a dog with heart, every time. Of course, Tom Lynch won the Produce Stakes with a one-eyed dog, Springvalley Grand. We have never had one of those although, Lord knows, we have had every other sort in the place."

FIGHTING: "I have an awful opinion that it is the heat which causes a lot of dogs to fight. They may also be getting too much racing; they may not be fully fit; or they may not be just right, injured in some way. You remember how my dog, Goldstar Mick, turned his head against Spargo in the semi-finals of the St Leger at Limerick. Well, it turned out he had done a toe in the race. My method with dogs that do fight — simply because it's in them — is to give them four or five solos. I believe that often works. I get a thrill out of training a dog that has fought, just for the challenge of getting it out of him — of taking him on."

GOING: "It is a matter in which you have to have patience. It would not cost me a thought to withdraw a dog if the going was wrong, either way. But there are owners who will insist on running their dogs. There are some dogs which love to have the track .20 slow; others like to hear their feet pounding. Many of the greyhounds which I have had will run as fast on going rated .20 or .30 slow as they would in good going. Oughter Brigg liked it slow, but most like a bit of give in the ground."

HEAT: "The one thing that kills dogs is heat and I would do anything to minimise its effects. Get a ventilator in the van; roll the windows down. I would sometimes get one of the lads to go into the side of the van, and let him sit there with the side-door open. The one problem about leaving the boot open is the exhaust fumes. There were times when you would see every dog in town going along with its head at the back and taking in the exhaust fumes. That was fine if you had a good travelling dog, if you did not you were in trouble."

INCONVENIENCE: "Always try and make sure they relieve themselves before putting them to bed. Most will not wet their bedding and that is the problem. They wait and wait until they are let out. It can be very damaging to the kidneys. The most extreme example was Nameless Star. If he wanted to relieve himself at night, he would just hang on. He would never wet the bedding. The only solution was to stay with him all the time. Many is the time that I stayed up with him all night."

JOURNEYS: "Many greyhounds suffer from travel sickness. I have found the best remedy is to put a chain at the back of the van to keep the dog still. I would never give travel sickness tablets. Another idea is to take the dog on car trips as often as possible when it is not racing, just for the ride. If you have a bitch travelling separately from the dogs, it is not a bad idea to bring another, non-racing, bitch along to keep her company. Never drive too hard with a dog that is inclined to be sick. I never drive hard, anyway. I couldn't travel in a bus for years. I kept thinking I was going to get sick. I suppose you get dogs which are much the same. All my greyhounds going to Britain travel by air, and the lads take over the van and all the necessaries on the boat."

KENNEL: "Sometimes we need to confine dogs, one to a kennel. Funnily enough, every dog by Whisper Wishes we have ever had in the place, we had to keep alone. In our experience, his progeny have tended to be sour and cross. That Bold Rabbit — now *there* was a bold bastard."

LIGHTS: "Getting a dog used to racing under lights is not the problem it used to be. With electricity everywhere nowadays, they soon adapt, but it could be difficult in the old days when we used lanterns in the yard. When they raced under lights at night, they wouldn't know where they were."

MATINGS: "Stud dogs can be a bit of a nuisance when you are running a racing kennel. They can get in the way and upset your other arrangement. And then there are other matters — like something which happened when we had Always Proud at stud. It was typical of the type of thing that breeders would get up to. Always Proud was standing at £50 and you gave back £10 'for luck'. Well, this fella rang and we agreed to give him the service for £20. The bitch did not have a good card but I just fancied she would breed something. Anyway, the £20 was agreed. Then the man arrived with his bitch by taxi and when he had got the service, he turned around and said that the taxi had been a little more expensive than he expected, £4 more in fact, and he handed me £16!"

NAMING: "We have had some dogs here with desperate names, and we have said: 'He just can't win with a name like that.' We've renamed a few. Moran's Beef comes to mind, I renamed him and it nearly got me into trouble. He was called Beaded Eagle when he came here, and I didn't fancy the name. It was not known that I had him, but then I rang up the Irish Coursing Club to change the name. Then it appeared in a corner of the *Sporting Press* under Changes In Names: Moran's Beef, and G. McKenna after it.

"When I rang Shelbourne Park to check about a bitch and what she was drawn against, I was told that she was in a graded race against

Moran's Beef! Of course, I had to tell the full-story — it was in the *Sporting Press* anyway — and I withdrew the bitch."

OWNING: "I have never owned a decent dog myself. But the lads have had some good ones. The trouble about training for your own sons is that you never get paid."

PUNTING: "I am not a great gambler but I have often had a couple of hundred quid on a dog. I'm the same with cards. We used to have a regular game here in the house. I often had a winning hand and there was a good pot; and I'd just throw in.

"You're a great man when you tip a winner, but not so great when you don't. Most of the owners are okay, and we have had some big gamblers. Most of them take it well if they get beaten. They understand what can happen. I know that there was a lot of money on Grove Whisper practically every night he ran. He won a lot of races at very short prices, but they just laid into him. In fact, he wasn't always the luckiest on the big night. I got one of my biggest thrills when he won the Paddy Whiskey Stakes in Youghal. He won by nine lengths. When he was right, he was just brilliant."

QUIETNESS: "We have a radio going full-blast in the kennels all day, although they can no longer be used in the kennels at the race tracks. At home we leave it on until 10 pm at night. It's mostly pop music, which the lads would rather listen to as well. It's not my taste."

RETIREMENT: "I have really never thought about it. I suppose eventually John, the eldest lad, will probably get a job outside the kennel. I suppose Ger and Owen will eventually get licences of their own."

SEEDING: "It's a good idea. It should have been used in Ireland long ago. But I would like to see a situation where races have three railers and three wide runners. There are men paying big money for dogs, and the way things are, you could have six seeded dogs in a race and your wide runner would get trap one. The three and three system, which I like, should be used at Wimbledon, more than anywhere."

TRIALS: "I would recommend confining good dogs to solo trials. It cuts down the chance of injury. I will never forget the year we had Knockrour Slave and Atlantic Expert at White City and they did not want to give us solo trials. Well, Atlantic Bridge was 150-1 and I knew he had a right chance, so I had a good few quid on him. We were of the opinion that Knockrour Slave should be on the outside, and they were all saying that he should be on the inside. So, out comes Knockrour Slave and cuts across. Atlantic Expert was knocked over, injured, out of the Derby."

UNLUCKIEST: "I have little doubt that Count Five was the unluckiest dog I ever trained."

VETERINARY: "I swear by Dr Muiris Drummy. There are some vets who haven't deserved their reputations. They would get about ten cases and do three good jobs, and everyone goes around saying how marvellous they are. But in fact, their rate of success was low."

WEIGHT: "It's a question of trial and error. I just look at a dog and have a fair idea what he should be. If you are in any doubt, race the dog a few times at varying weights, and see how things turn out. You can gauge by their improvement, or otherwise, as to what their correct weight should be."

"Prince of Bermuda was the worst example I have seen. They were racing him at seventy-two pounds and I instantly knew he was about five pounds too heavy. He eventually raced for us at around sixty-seven pounds. But it is hard to say how you would know exactly. Clean them out, vomit them out, and then see how they settle down. If the dog is not running well, adjust his weight."

XYZ: "Yes, there are any number of other things which can change my way of thinking. They are just superstitions, plain and simple. Like not wearing green. In fact, I hate to see it and wouldn't want to be with a person wearing anything green, especially on the night of a final. And, of course, I hate to meet a funeral on the road. I didn't see anyone wearing green, and I didn't come across a funeral on the night that Lartigue Note won. All day, everything was going right."

CHAPTER TWELVE

Coursing

WHEN greyhound racing started, track dogs were not going to simply materialise. Coursing dogs — the only dogs there were — became track dogs. The wonder is that they adapted so well to their new surroundings, to chasing a mechanical lure. Maybe it was because they were coursing dogs — real dogs getting real courses and real turns — that they took to it so well and were so genuine. Many would say that this is why the current track dogs are soft, a great number of them, anyway. They are not genuinely pursuing the hare at the track because they have never been run after the real thing. Some have never seen a hare and some are by parents which have never seen, nor coursed, a live hare. Ger McKenna believes this is why the breeding of many of his recent winners is very mixed. McKenna has taken the unfashionably-bred and turned them into champions.

"It is because some of the established dogs are throwing nothing," he says. "Their pups are useless. There are so many dogs around which are not genuine. They have no heart. You just have to take them as they come. See how they run. If they are genuine in themselves, then you take them and train them."

The changeover was not intentional, but nowadays the good track dog never courses. They are just too valuable to be risked up an uneven field, used for running greyhounds but once a year. It is a comparatively recent phenomenon. From 1927 and up to fifty years later, all greyhounds were dual purpose.

"At that time all track dogs coursed," McKenna remembers. "You coursed them and then they went to the track. That was the order. The tracks were closed in November and they didn't open again until the

Ger and sons Owen and Ger after Top Price had won the Lough Suedy Cup, 1981.

Ger with Choice of Litter, winner of Corn na Gaillimhe at the Galway/Oranmore coursing meeting.

Saturday after the National Meeting in Clonmel. I still think they should be closed in winter. In December and January at least. We are simply not geared for winter racing in Ireland."

McKenna rates Move Handy (Dandy Man — Move Sally) as his best coursing dog. As fast as Irish Rain on the track, the dog won the McAlevey Gold Cup at East Donegal when only a duffer and was one of the McKenna charges to lift the Mayo United Cup at Ballina. Move Handy capped his coursing career by running up the all-aged Champion Stakes at Clonmel's National Meeting to Rusheen Gallant. McKenna remembers the dog's owner Martin Hogan from nearby Cloughjordan, Co. Tipperary, with affection.

"I remember it was the year that Move Gas won the National Sprint and we were coming home from the other Belfast track, Celtic Park. I remember that I had had two winners that night; one of them was Portumna Wonder (Wonder Valley — Useless Light), which was owned by Barney Curley.

"Martin wasn't feeling well at the track, and on the way home he was saying that he felt unwell again. He got out of the car at Banbridge, Co. Down — about half-way between Belfast and the Border. He seemed to be okay again and then he just died. He was sixty-one — I think it was his heart. I seemed to be taking it okay. But then after a couple of days it hit me badly."

McKenna's Irish National Sprint winner, Bauhus (Solar Prince — Lovely Sister), lifted the Cork Cup at Blarney in 1964 and 1965; but Choice of Litter (Glittering Look — Maggie's Choice) holds a place in both the coursing honours lists and the hearts of a young couple. The owner was a Charleville, Co. Cork, farmer, Anthony Watson.

"He was the best judge of a greyhound I ever knew and the decentest fella I ever had anything to do with," says McKenna.

In 1960 the Galway and Oranmore meeting was held over the Christmas period. It was St Stephen's Night and Choice of Litter was still going strong in Corn na Gaillimhe. But the trainer was anxious, as any young man would be in his situation.

"That was the night we had arranged that I should go down to Birr and be introduced to Josie's parents," he recalls.

Josie's father had no interest in dogs, but the impression made by the polite lad was undoubtedly cemented when he could boast a day later that Choice of Litter had won the Cup at Galway. Choice of Litter went on to win the Mayo United Cup at Ballina, where they no longer have a fixture, but which was a favourite with McKenna at the time. Albert Lucas' Proud Lincoln, yet another of Clonalvy Pride's progeny, was one of McKenna's top dogs. Without question, he was his outstanding all-purpose greyhound.

"We had nothing done with him," says the trainer, "maybe just a trial or two in Shelbourne Park. But we qualified him at Loughrea and his owner was anxious to run him at the National Meeting. He was just beaten by Potipher in the last stride in a semi-final course in which there was no turn."

Later in 1967, he went one better on the track at Harold's Cross when he reached the final of the Irish Derby. But Proud Lincoln was badly baulked and it was Tom Lynch's Russian Gun, which he had beaten previously, which took the premier track prize. Proud Lincoln returned to Harold's Cross in 1968 and ran a sparkling 29.16 for 525 yards to win the Callanan Cup and moved across to Shelbourne Park where he took the Cambridgeshire over 600 yards in a time of 33.72. Irish Rain (Wonder Valley — Sonny's Gift), which McKenna trained for Martin Divilly, was unfortunate in that his puppy year was 1968 when he would have probably started favourite for the Clonmel Derby. But it was the year of the Foot and Mouth Disease outbreak and no National Meeting was held. But, again, he went on to win the Mayo United Cup, Westmeath United's Belsize Cup at Killucan, the Connacht Cup at Loughrea and run up Corn na Gaillimhe. He was a greyhound of which McKenna thought a great deal. He ran a then track record of 23.60 first time around at Dunmore Stadium but he was on the burly side for the summer game and suffered from bad toes.

With the exception of Own Pride — which achieved the quite unique feat of defeating a future coursing Derby winner in Tender Heather in 1969 before going on himself to win Ireland's Blue Riband of the track — and his Waterloo Cup participation, there is then a virtual break in the McKenna coursing record. In the Seventies, Irish greyhound racing was to reach new heights of popularity. A new emphasis on marketing saw total attendances in the Republic rise to 725,000 in 1960 when McKenna won his second classic and second Irish St Leger with Swanlands Best, and level out at 804,733 in 1969 in the year that Own Pride gave him his first Irish Derby and brought his classic total into double figures. While attendances were on the decline in Britain, crowds in Ireland were about to surge and they peaked at 1,074,687 in 1975 and also passed through the magic million mark the following season. The graph was fairly level into the next decade and, logically, as crowds grew, so did sponsorship, prize money and betting. The price and value of greyhounds kept pace. It was unthinkable that dogs, with asking prices of £60,000 — in some cases — as racers and potentially worth many more times that as stud prospects, would be allowed to course when the richest prize of all, the Derby, was worth much less than its current £10,000 until recently. With the coursing season so short at five months, McKenna logically concentrated on the track.

"You just can't do as many coursing dogs as you can for the track. There is a lot more work involved," he says. Coursing dogs need constant galloping and up to eight miles road-work per day. They can be a nuisance in a lot of ways and the coursing dogs are so big these days. You would hardly be seen on a coursing field in Ireland now with a dog less than 90 pounds weight.

"But Owen, in particular, loves the coursing and I am starting to think more in terms of coursing myself again. It would help if they put the National Meeting back a bit to the end of February. We are presently keeping five coursing dogs in the kennels — three pups and two all-ages — and we would hope to keep at least that number in future."

January 1989 saw Ger McKenna in a classic dilemma, the type that makes him unable to combine the field and track aspects as he would like. Already successful for McKenna in the all-age at Westport, Sean McLoughney's Razor's Best (Duffer's Ranger — Razor Sharp) was entered at Millstreet for the North Cork Cup. She was still there at the end of day one, but the hot favourite, Kerryman Teddy Buckley's Village Bess (Ballyduff Boy — Hammond Bess) was in the same, bottom half of the draw. Razor's Best dealt with her sister Flashy Riona, owned by the breeder Hubert Heffernan, New Inn, Co. Tipperary, and looked destined to meet Village Bess. But showing the tendency which she had in the previous round on the first day, Village Bess, after displaying awesome speed, ran past the hare which was only inches from her. The way clear, Razor's Best beat All That Crack in the semi-finals and Mathematics in the decider. His job done, McKenna rushed off to prepare Tomijo for the Sporting Life Juvenile Championship at Wimbledon. But he was impressed by the pup Village

Bess and, likewise, her owner had not lost sight of the fact that McKenna had trained the eventual winner. It was agreed that McKenna would prepare Village Bess for the coursing Oaks. An early problem arose when she showed signs of going into season.

"It is something which I am most reluctant to do, but we gave her medication to stop her breaking down," says Ger. "We really had no choice. You only get one chance at the Oaks. I was also worried about her travelling to the coursing every day so we decided to stay nearer Clonmel. We went down a week before the meeting, just to make sure she had time to settle into her new surroundings."

The talking dogs of this Oaks were Davy Reynolds' Sceal Eile, the 7-2 favourite, John Joe O'Keeffe's Redundant Pal and Michael O'Donovan's Swing Out Sister, which went off joint second favourites at 6-1. But the word was out that McKenna had Village Bess, and her odds were soon cut to 7-1. By day two, Sceal Eile had gone out and the other three were still standing. However, Village Bess had taken a full cartwheel of a tumble which would be a minus factor in the open at Altcar, but would be looked upon as an insurmountable handicap at the enclosed version. But Village Bess, her kinks ironed-out — she showed no reluctance to go into the hare, nor was she ever in danger of going unsighted after being prepared for Clonmel by McKenna — was still there at the end of the second day.

Village Bess made her exit from Powerstown Park in the semi-finals of the Oaks after a just-up decision went in favour of Swing Out Sister which had her nose in front as the hare veered. It was a memorable buckle, arguably the best of the whole three days. Village Bess had not won the coursing Oaks. But from being a misfit which was doing everything wrong less than a month previously, she had been transformed to the extent that she rated and coursed with the elite of her sex at the sport's top end-of-season showpiece. Ger McKenna had shown that whether it be in track or field, he is the Maestro.

CHAPTER THIRTEEN

The Waterloo Cup

GER McKenna lives a full day, a full year. He is up first thing in the morning and is sometimes not in bed until the early hours of the next day. His life is greyhounds. Totally. Three-hundred and sixty-five days of the year. Ger McKenna does not drink alcohol. Never has. In a country where it is the main and, in some parts still, the only social outlet, many would view his existence as almost ascetic. He was a heavy smoker once.

"I remember — and I wasn't that young at the time — that I was smoking and I didn't realise that my father knew I smoked. Then one night we were at the dogs and he turned around and offered me one. I nearly dropped. A few years later, I must have been smoking forty or more a day at that stage, I went to the yard one morning. I used to start smoking first thing and I took a cigarette out of the box. I looked at it, and then just went and threw the whole packet into the river."

Ger likes a pipe of tobacco in the evening when the conversation is about greyhounds, greyhound owners, hurling . . . and back to greyhounds. His only addiction is tea. "Would you like a cup of tea, Jo?" he asks by way of letting Josie know that he is ready for the next brewing. The previous pot was made ten minutes earlier. Josie longs for a holiday. Just the two of them.

"I have been to Canada a couple of times to see my sister," she says. "But we have never had a holiday on our own, so to speak."

One sees Ger as an unwilling holidaymaker: "I sometimes think I would like to go to Brighton . . . and take in the track!"

Where else? It is impossible to imagine him on the beach, in the deckchair with the trousers rolled up and the knotted handkerchief on his head. The boys will take a break. John went to London with his girlfriend and had a good time. "We went to Walthamstow and Wimbledon and . . ."

Ger senior will not. The Spring is the time that you find out what you have in your kennel — sprinting at Shelbourne Park. The summer belongs to Wimbledon — the English Derby. The autumn is Ireland — and the Derby and St Leger. The winter is coursing . . .

"God but I hate it," says Josie. "We went a good few years without a coursing dog. Now Ger is getting more interested, we have it all over again. All those sandwiches to make, all the wet gear and muddy boots when they come home."

The consolation is the Waterloo Cup. "Well, I suppose it's the closest to a holiday that we are ever likely to get," says Josie.

The Waterloo Cup is more than an anachronism. It is both out of place and out of time. It delightfully ignores eight hundred years of hostility between the landed English and peasant Irish. For more than a century and a half Altcar has been common ground for two nationalities; two classes. It is a rightly revered greyhound and social institution. For Ger McKenna, his family steeped in the annals of the longtails, his own life running on parallel lines with the very history of greyhound racing, the event and the place have a natural, instinctive draw. In contradiction to the way in which they might have been regarded by previous Waterloo Cup generations, the Irish have what amounts to a sense of superiority when it comes to the Blue Riband of the Leash. The Irish greyhound is faster and — no matter what the judge says — that is what matters to them. If you cannot lead the English dog, not just by a specified margin, but by half the field, then your dog is no good. Go home. The lips clamp down on the pipe. An uneasy shift in the chair. McKenna looks towards the window, although he knows there is nothing there to see. There is just a suggestion of a blush in the cheeks:

"Well, yes. I sold him to the gypsies and they won it with him the next year."

The place is Lydiate and, traditionally, it is *the* testing ground. The Irish may have been faster the first day, but the English will soften them up here. Bared of spectators, it is hard to visualise it on the second day of the Cup. Fill the car park, put up the tents and line the bank with eager enthusiasts and it is the sport at its purest. This is *the* test. They crane their necks, struggle to balance on the ditch to watch every weave and turn. Vantage points are few. But the groans and cheers tell the unsighted how the course is progressing — a turn, a wrench, a go-by; all are visible through the sounds of the crowd. The course can last for minutes. Dogs, their initial exuberance wasted by the chase, lob along after the fleeing hare. They are not even scoring at this point. But they still go on after the judge has raised his flag. In the third round of the 1972 Cup, Captain J.H. Chadwick had no doubt that Eightsome Reel had out-pointed Modest Newdown (Newdown Heather — Modest Millie). Oblivious to his elimination, Modest Newdown — described by coursing correspondent, later keeper of the English Stud Book Charles Blanning, as "irascible in temperament, and almost impossible to catch after his course" made for the sough, his panting training Ger McKenna in his wake. Showing typical impishness, McKenna commandeered a local farmer and his tractor and headed in pursuit.

"Modest Newdown had been run into the ground and when we came back on the tractor I was only too happy when a Mr Lee offered to buy him for £200. He was, after all, a second season dog which had been gruelled."

William Lee, a Romany dealer, sent Modest Newdown to Mary Birbeck who had just started training in Norfolk.

"I went over the next year with the intention of backing him," says McKenna. "I often went when I didn't have a runner. I was going to have a tenner or a score on him, just in case. But I got no encouragement. I heard he was running terrible."

The Waterloo Cup roll of honour shows that in 1973, a year after being sold by Ger McKenna, Mr W. Lee's Modest Newdown won the premier prize in coursing.

Mckenna retorts: "You can only hope for the best at Altcar. The man who tells you that he is going to win the Waterloo Cup should be in an asylum."

The energy of Sir Mark Prescott, heading a new style committee, made sure that the Waterloo Cup — first run in 1836 — not only survived in the 1980's (it had not been run for the three years 1978–80) but prospered. The English would run it. The Irish would sustain it. Pat and Monita Holland's Play Solo won the Cup in 1982 and Brian Divilly's Little Shoe won the Plate in this year and the next. The recipe was an old one. A pacey Irish dog, which had won a trial stake, but gone out early at the National Meeting at Clonmel; or a dog which had shaped up well in a trial stake. This is what the majority brought with which to win the Waterloo Cup. Bill Gaskin, the Waterloo Cup nominator, telephoned McKenna before the 1984 coursing classic to see if the trainer could secure him a dog capable of winning the Cup. The deadline was approaching and Gaskin, anxious to know, rang back.

"I remember Ger going to the phone and telling Bill. There was a long silence at the other end," Josie McKenna recalls.

Gaskin was speechless. McKenna had got him a bitch — and bitches did not win the Waterloo Cup. Tubbertelly Queen, owned by Terry McCann who originally comes from Tubbercurry, and Pat Kilcoyne from the same Co. Sligo town, had made it to the Clonmel Oaks semi-finals as a puppy. The McKenna connection was strong on the Kilcoyne side. The two families are close and Pat Kilcoyne's father Luke, a superb Irish Cup slipper up to his retirement earlier in the decade, was later to become a member of both the Irish Coursing Club Executive and Bord na gCon. McKenna is modest about his direct involvement with Tubbertelly Queen's (Scotch Lundy — Miss Queenie) 1984 success.

"I recommended her as a runner, but I just happened to be there at the time. I gave a hand but Pat Kilcoyne did it all."

Charles Blanning recorded that Tubbertelly Queen had won "shattering in the process all kinds of records: she became the first Irish bitch since Honeymoon in 1875 to win, the first bitch to win since Golden Surprise in 1929 and the first favourite to win since Roving Minstrel in 1850."

Altogether, she was an inspired choice. The mould had been broken. The next year, 1985, another young trainer Michael O'Donovan from Tipperary Town, a protege of Ronnie Chandler, came over with Hear and There and won the final against Stephen Stack's Morning Lass. Again Blanning provided the historic significance: "They were the first bitch puppies to reach the decider since Bit of Fashion and Miss Glendyne exactly a century earlier, and Hear and There was the first of her age and sex to triumph since Snowflight in 1882."

The Waterloo Cup, weather permitting, runs Tuesday to Thursday, and McKenna sets out on Sunday for the Colburn kennels in Liverpool.

"I have always gone there with the dogs. I knew the father, John, well," he says. "It is the only time when the dogs do not go by plane. We take them over in the van, by boat, as it is such a short run over."

The McKennas stay in Southport, which is within easy access of the coursing fields. Constantly learning and experimenting, the man who had provoked the bitch revival, changed direction again in 1987 — the Cup had been called off in 1986 because of frost. McKenna brought over Chagall — and everybody laughed. At least, McKenna felt they were all laughing.

"Well, I had good reason to believe it," he says. "I was in the Scarisbrook Hotel in Southport on the night before the start when they have the callover of odds, and this Irish fella, who according to himself knows a lot of about things, came up and said: 'Why did you bring that joke with you?' "

McKenna liked the dog; and he liked the name even if the pronounciation had been corrupted on most lips to be Shagall. Chagall (Duffer's Ranger — Smokey Flavour) had won the all-aged at Tubbercurry and was formerly owned by John Kelly and trained by John Quigley, who had a host of good coursing dogs and whose track successes include the Irish National Sprint with Autumn Magic (1986) and the Irish Derby with Make History (1988). Ironically, like many dogged coursing men, Kelly confesses to have little, if any interest in the track. But he knows his coursing dogs and many assumed that, when he was willing to sell, there must be nothing left in Chagall. McKenna trained him for Ernest Smith, a great enthusiast, and one of the driving forces behind his club in the Isle of Wight. Smith had only one ambition in mind and that was to win the Waterloo Cup. McKenna, these days more anxious than ever to do the same thing, put the dog away to get him fresh.

"After all that had been said, it gave me one of the biggest thrills when he got to the final," he says. "I never said it before, but when we went to collect him on the morning of the last day, we found that he was off-colour. He had scoured all over the place. Later on, he was even passing signs of blood. All we could really do at that stage was to give him brandy and port to warm him up. I felt that we had to go on. Chagall was, without a shadow of a doubt, the fastest dog in the competition and we just had to pray that he would keep going."

Although the danger signals were there for those observing his running, Chagall got over his penultimate hurdle. But in the decider he

Owen with his father's Chagall goes to slips with Mousetail for the final of the 1987 Waterloo Cup.

had nothing left to give; his sickness finally took its toll as he was decisively led by Mousetail. Chagall, his earlier speed making him favourite to win out, showed heart and scored a few subsequent points before the hare made cover. Mousetail's owners Michael and June Collins were, like Chagall's Ernest Smith, from the Isle of Wight and helped him revive the tiny coursing club there. McKenna had started it all by recommending that Bill Gaskin nominate Tubbertelly Queen. Mousetail became the third Irish-bred bitch on the trot to win the Waterloo Cup and Michael and June were the first English owners to train a winner of the Blue Riband since Mutual Friend in 1959. McKenna, the spectator, had supported the Waterloo Cup for many years in the old days. McKenna, the trainer, had revolutionised it in the new era. But he had yet to win it. After Chagall he said: "I'll never win the Waterloo Cup, now he hasn't won."

Whether you are on The Withins on the first and third day, or at Lydiate, sandwiched in-between — coursing at Altcar can be murder. The cold is something which the Irish, spoiled by the North Atlantic Drift and unused to such extremes, find the hardest. Their dogs suffer too. They have all, naturally, been up a coursing field. But home was never like this. Home is park coursing. One quick turn and you are finished, and sometimes there might not even be one turn. There is no waiting in slips. Brian Divilly had great hopes for Crafty Autumn and she went off a restricted 6-1 favourite to win the 1989 Waterloo Cup. But she was left waiting and waiting on the second morning at Lydiate and she went out.

Divilly concludes: "The cold got to her."

It is not the only danger. There are drains, filled with a black viscous substance. Fionntra Felon (Scotch Lundy — Irish Melody) was Ger McKenna's most recent attempt to win the Waterloo Cup. Ernest Smith took the dog on and in the first round of the all-aged at Ennisworthy, he ran well against Central Cee Bee, the previous season's Irish Cup runner-up. Enniscorthy is a handkerchief of a field, even in park coursing terms, and when a bye situation occurred in the next round, Fionntra Felon went back up again and not only won readily, but showed determination when going into the hare. Altcar — here we come! Lydiate, with its vastness, its cold and its drains, kills off the opposition and when Fionntra Felon beat Stephen Stack's Knockdown Solo to get to the semi-finals, he was immediately made odds-on favourite to win out. The dog had fallen in a drain and been worked as hard as the others, but he went back to Liverpool no more tired than his opponents, and the Irish retired to Southport joyfully anticipating a win on the concluding day. The car park was practically empty, early on the day at The Withins. McKenna's van stood in isolation in the middle. Only the ashen face of young Owen McKenna told there was something wrong. Ger was quiet.

"I'm sorry Ger," said Sir Mark Prescott, stuck for words the way you are when confronted by the family of the deceased at a funeral.

What can you say to a man bereaved, who has to withdraw the favourite from the Cup just two steps away from immortality. The words will be inadequate, sound inadequate, anyway. Ger and Owen had driven to Liverpool that morning. When they opened his kennel, Fionntra Felon had scoured all over the place. Just like Chagall.

"He must have swallowed whole mouthfuls of stuff in the drain," was Ger's verdict. His words after Chagall's defeat had come back to haunt the man who must carry on: "I'll never win the Waterloo cup, now he hasn't won."

CHAPTER FOURTEEN

The Maestro

THE daily newspapers in Ireland give greyhounds adequate coverage. Adequate; but no more. Editors, by and large, do not think positively about what is an industry as much as a sport. It takes something out of the ordinary to enable the dogs to command a prominent place on the page. More often than not, it is Ger McKenna who provides the material; the story. When the Maestro won his second English Derby, with Lartigue Note, now that *was* news. It lifted the greyhound section from an off-page. It also made Ger McKenna a recipient of the Jury's Hotel–Irish Independent Sportstar of the Week Award. The presentation took place in Dublin. McKenna was happy and relaxed, in the company of Josie and one of their owners Pat Leamy. The conversation turned to Vincent O'Brien — the Ger McKenna of horse racing. We recalled how at one time everything went right for Vincent O'Brien. Now he was struggling. In the way that such things happen, one calamity was followed by another. He was going through a rough patch. O'Brien had sought to finance the stocking of his stable by going public in late 1987. But after a bright opening, Saratogen flopped in the English 2,000 Guineas at Newmarket and the value of shares in Classic Thoroughbreds plc had bottomed out at 16 pence. McKenna was philosophical. It could happen to anyone . . . to him.

In the high summer of 1989 all attention was focused on Lartigue Note's next race. McKenna had given warning that his lightly-raced black dog was in line for the Irish Derby. But the non-stop sunshine which was a boon for the Tourist Board, was a catastrophe for the greyhound trainer. Even those looking forward to the coursing season two-and-a-half months away were worried. Even if the rain came, they would hardly have time to get their charges ready for October. It meant trouble for Ger McKenna. It was less than a month since the English Derby and Lartigue Note was desperately short of a trial. The immediate objective was the Carrolls International 525. The Dundalk feature has seeding and Lartigue Note's chances looked good. But McKenna decided that the dog had to get the work and so he took him to Errill schooling track.

"I walked it beforehand and was happy about the trial," says Ger. "I cannot blame the owner of the schooling track. It is well-kept and had been well-watered."

The irony was that Lartigue Note had finished his trial, had done his 300 yard spin and was in the back straight again.

"I knew immediately," said McKenna. Lartigue Note had broken his hock.

"That's far from trouble," said Josie McKenna. "That's the way Ger looks at it. If something happens to one of the boys, then that's trouble. But as long as it stays outside the house . . . Of course, it was a big disappointment. For the lads and for us all. We were lucky that Cathal McCarthy owns the dog. He has horses and he knows the way things go." There are compensations. Angelo Carlotti, in his first race for McKenna, wins the £1,200 Purina 500 in 28.12, equalling the track record. But there are no certainties. The following night, Wednesday, August 16, Pat Leamy's Heather's Best (Ramtogue Champ — Lucky Signal), the fastest greyhound to run a Shelbourne Park sprint since Lauragh Six and the McKenna-trained ante-post favourite for the Respond Irish Derby, chipped a bone in a trial and had to be withdrawn from the classic. Yet the fairytale hopes of finishing the season with an English and Irish Derby winner were not over. Attractive Son had been the forgotten dog in Ger's bid to win the English Derby. Overlooked in the thousands of words which described the feat of Lartigue Note in winning at Wimbledon was the fact that for much of the marathon competition, Attractive Son was going equally well. Owned by Jim Hayes, from Knocklong, Co. Limerick, who has extensive business interests around the Wimbledon area, Attractive Son got to the quarter-finals, when he was eliminated, the victim of being drawn in trap five, when he wanted the rails. Again, Attractive Son was overshadowed in the prelude to the Irish Derby. Lartigue Note had

Ger and 1989 English Derby winner Lartigue Note.   *Steve Nash*

broken his hock. Lodge Prince had done a wrist and Heather's Best — generally regarded as McKenna's main Irish premier classic contender — was out as well.

It was an historic and much-debated Irish Derby. The Irish are a traditional lot and plenty was made of the double introduction of seeding and an even more talked-about points system. Attractive Son rode both hurdles. He failed to win in just one round but qualified easily even in defeat, and he negotiated one of his victories from trap four. Suddenly — or so it seemed — Attractive Son was in the final of the £30,000 Respond Irish Derby. But nobody, especially his trainer, was concealing the fact that he needed trap one to be in with a realistic chance of toppling the unbeaten Manorville Magic, one of the hottest favourites for years. It was like old times. Two years previously, Josie McKenna had come to the draw knowing that she had to pick out trap six to give Rathgallen Tady a life. Now she prayed for trap one. There was silence; and trap three made the silence almost audible. It is never a good draw but, the problem was to be compounded by the fact that Yes Speedy, designated as a wide-runner in Britain but, for some reason, deemed a railer here, was in trap two. Guinness Irish National Sprint winner Mac's Lock, in one, looked sure to lead; Dereen Star, to the right of Attractive Son, would probably move in. It can be truthfully said that Attractive Son was the only greyhound which genuinely needed the rails, and yet he was right in the middle. The trap draw had meant a lot this time — just as it had for Rathgallen Tady. It just did not work out.

Ger forced a smile at the weigh-in. Nobody, perhaps not even he, would ever be so close to winning the English and Irish Derby with different greyhounds in the same year. They lined up: Tom Fox's Mac's Lock (Quare Rocket — Killetra Queen); the Eddie Costello-owned, John McGee-trained Yes Speedy (Curryhills Fox — Yes Mam); Ger McKenna's Jim Hayes-owned Attractive Son (Very Attractive — Ballinamona Mum); Dan and Jim O'Driscoll's Matt O'Donnell-trained Dereen Star (Moral Support — Summer Crab); Melvin Hamilton's Glenhill Jack (Iran Jack — Disco Clare); Mrs Catherine Doran's Manorville Magic (Manorville Sand — Black Vision). As the only wide runner in the new-look Shelbourne Park showpiece, Manorville Magic went off as even money favourite followed by 4-1 Dereen Star, 6-1 Mac's Lock and Yes Speedy, 7-1

The McKenna family: (pictured left to right) Owen (Heather's Best), Josie (Annacurra Hill), Ger (Attractive Son) and grandson Kevin, John (Angelo Carlotti) and Ger jnr (Tomijo).   Steve Nash

Attractive Son and 16-1 Glenhill Jack. It was a famous Derby final and the most thrilling that most of the packed attendance had ever witnessed. True to form, Mac's Lock went off in front. But they queued up behind to take his place. Yes Speedy was on his tail but was also depriving Attractive Son of the rails. Manorville Magic was at the back of the field with Glenhill Jack, and Dereen Star had been baulked at the first turn. As they rounded for home, Mac's Lock still had the advantage. But, as they neared the line, his stamina was running out. Yes Speedy, too, appeared to have given his all. In an instant, Attractive Son loomed on the outside. But he was still trying for the rails even at this late stage. In what was to prove the crucial factor, Attactive Son was held up sufficiently so that Manorville Magic slipped by on the rails. Technically, it was a five-way photograph, something which is unprecedented in an Irish Derby final. But those on the line had no doubt that Manorville Magic had just got up to deny Mac's Lock, with Attractive Son third. A fabulous final, and so nearly a famous, fairytale finish.

But when you have been in the game for forty years, you get a sense of perspective. In this decade alone, Ger McKenna-trained greyhounds have contested one hundred and forty-five finals and feature races. He baulks at the idea of naming his greatest greyhounds, they all have their memories, and their owners have their sensitivities. In a rare moment of revelation, McKenna agrees to compile a list of eighteen of his top greyhounds — the number that would be in the three semi-finals of the Irish Derby. He has to imagine that he has available to him all his great dogs, since Prince of Bermuda in 1956 up to Lartigue Note in 1989 that ran over 525 yards at Shelbourne Park.

McKenna picks the eighteen: Ballybeg Prim, Ballykilty, Ballroughan, Bashful Man, Bold Rabbit, Count Five, Grove Whisper, Itsachampion, Knockrour Slave, Lartigue Note, Moran's Beef, Nameless Pixie, Own Pride, Parkdown Jet, Prince of Bermuda, Shamrock Point, Time up Please, Yanka Boy.

Josie and Owen are enthusiastic. Ger is not. But we make the draw with Ger doing the seeding.

First semi-final: 1. Nameless Pixie; 2. Shamrock Point; 3. Knockrour Slave (w); 4. Parkdown Jet (w); 5. Bashful Man (w); 6. Moran's Beef (w).

Summary: It is McKenna's opinion that, given this draw, Bashful Man would get first run on his opponents. Parkdown Jet and Knockrour Slave would go around the bend second and third but at the finish, Bashful Man would just hold on from Nameless Pixie, which has not got the early pace but has picked them off on the way home.

Second semi-final: 1. Grove Whisper; 2. Time Up Please; 3. Lartigue Note; 4. Bold Rabbit (w); 5. Prince of Bermuda (w); 6. Yanka Boy (w).

Summary: Lartigue Note would get enough space down the centre and just get the bend on the rails in front of Grove Whisper. The latter would stick with Lartigue Note which, however, would stay on the stronger.

Third semi-final: 1. Itsachampion; 2. Own Pride; 3 Ballybeg Prim; 4. Ballyroughan (w); 5. Count Five (w); 6. Ballykilty (w).

Summary: Ballykilty, with a superb record from six, would trap best and win handily from the staying-on Itsachampion.

Final line-up

1. Mr Cathal McCarthy's Lartigue Note bk.d (One To Note — Lartigue Spark, July '87). Best form line: Won English Derby, 480m Wimbledon: 28.79.
2. Miss Deirdre Hynes' Itsachampion bk.d. (Monalee Champion —

Cranog Bet, November '70). Best form line: Won Guinness 600y Shelbourne Park: 33.45.

3. Mrs Rita McCauley's Nameless Pixie bk.b (Monalee Champion — Itsastar, July '77). Best form line: Won Irish Oaks, 525y Harold's Cross: 29.34.

4. Mr Tony Brennan's Grove Whisper f.d. (Whisper Wishes — Grove Road, February '85). Best form line: Won Anglo-Irish International, 550y. Shelbourne Park: 30.43.

5. Miss Deirdre Hynes' Bashful Man (w) bk.d. (Myross Again — Ballyflake, June' 71). Best form line: Won Irish Derby, 525y, Shelbourne Park: 28.82.

6. Mr Eamonn Gaynor's Ballykilty (w) w.bd.d. (Always Proud — Kitty True, June '69). Best form line: Won semi-final Irish Derby, 525y Shelbourne Park: 29.14.

Summary: The draw, made by his wife, had decided it for trainer Ger McKenna. Lartigue Note, one of four inside runners, is just where he wants to be, on the rails. With Itsachampion and Nameless Pixie on his outside, Lartigue Note would easily get the bend here. For all his alacrity from the outside, Ballykilty would not hold Bashful Man and the latter would move into second place. With Nameless Pixie again leaving it that bit too late, she would finish third. "With that draw I do not believe that Lartigue Note could have been beaten," says Ger. "I would have thought he would win such a final in around 28.90."

It is a game, a theoretical exercise, but it shows something of the unique understanding that McKenna has for his greyhounds. It may seem that the man they call the Maestro has nothing left to win, that all his ambitions have been fulfilled. He could look back on a career of unparalleled success and bask in the glory of simply being the best. But that is not the way of Ger McKenna. For him, every dog is an individual, and so every dog is a challenge. As long as there are greyhounds in his kennels, there is work to be done — and the great McKenna is in his prime.

Appendix I

Breeding

AS much as Prince of Bermuda played an integral role in the development of Ger McKenna the trainer, so Clonalvy Pride is the breeding cornerstone in his story. The son of Solar Prince — which was a Champion Prince dog — out of Asmena, represents the cream of breeding of his age. Clonalvy Pride was the grand-sire of Own Pride, the first Ger McKenna-trained Irish Derby winner, and his influence stretches down to his debut English Derby winner Parkdown Jet, right through to his most recent Blue Riband winner Lartigue Note. Clonalvy Pride went to the final of the 1960 English Derby in which he finished last; but he won the Pall Mall at Harringay and then took the English Laurels at Wimbledon in 1961, the year in which he completed a classic double by taking the English St Leger at Wembley. Clonalvy Pride was an outstanding race dog and proved exceptional at stud. Most importantly from a McKenna point of view, he sired Yanka Boy and Always Proud which, in turn, got Own Pride. The two branches join in the mating of Cairnville Jet (Own Pride — Cairnville Bet) and Gabriel Ruby (Peruvian Style — Gabriel Blue). Ruby's dam Gabriel Ruby is by Yanka Boy out of Gabriel Star. This produced Parkdown Jet and his sister Gabriel Doll, dam to Lartigue Spark, who went on to produce Lartigue Note.

Thus, there is a very close connection between Lartigue Note, Parkdown Jet and Own Pride, three Ger McKenna-trained Derby winners; and various other branches of the same breeding have given the Borrisokane, Co. Tipperary, handler numerous classic and feature winners. Examples include Nameless Pixie. Her sire Monalee Champion crops up on both sides of the breeding of Lartigue Note, as grand-sire of Cairnville Jet and One To Note. Nameless Pixie's dam Itsastar was by Yanka Boy (ex Itsamint). Itsastar is also dam of Nameless Star from her mating to Rita's Choice. So again, as with the Irish Derby, the ties between Gay McKenna, who trained Always Proud and Rita's Choice, and his country cousin are strong in the stud area. Yanka Boy, apart from crediting Ger McKenna with two of his thirty-two classics, gave him Ballymaclune, third in the English Derby, and he, in turn sired Sweeping Bally which threw McKenna's Irish Laurels winner Back Garden. Yanka Boy comes right up to date as grand-sire of Grove Road, dam of Grove Whisper. Itsachampion (Monalee Champion — Cranog Bet) is a brother of Cairnville Bet, grand-dam of Parkdown Jet. The underlying fact is that Ger McKenna, while getting the best out of greyhounds as racers, has done this to such effect that it has not impaired their stud potential.

Prince Of Bermuda
Bd. dog, August '53

CHAMPION PRINCE	Bellas Prince	Castledown Lad	Meadow Fescue
			Tender Cutlet
		Bellas Witch	Bellas Brother
			Noted Witch
	Sallywell	Swanky Jog	All Together
			Short O Dough
		Lucy Lilla	Orluck
			Lisdaleen
SUNORA	Darcel	Ruby Border	Creamery Border
			Keel Ruby
		City Dance	Top Of Cork Road
			Rattling Florrie
	Cute Fanny	Highland Rum	Rum Ration
			Liagh Lady
		Sandy Fanny	White Sandills
			Fanny Bunty

Ballkilty
W.bd. dog, June '69

ALWAYS PROUD	Clonalvy Pride	Solar Prince	Champion Prince
			Lisabelle
		Asmena	Westbury Sammy
			Leading Lady
	Always A Rebel	Ollys Quare Rebel	Riverdale Rebel
			Quare Fire
		Always Knitting	Bellas Prince
			Ashgrove Breeze
KITTY TRUE	Crazy Parachute	Hi There	Slaney Record
			Dublin Red
		Mad Prospect	Mad Tanist
			Caledonian Desire
	Ballykinlar Gem	Irish Quarter	Champion Prince
			Big Bawn
		Clohenbeg Dancer	Atomic Line
			Dancing Smart

Itsachampion
Bk. dog, Nov '70

MONALEE CHAMPION	Crazy Parachute	Hi There	Slaney Record
			Dublin Red
		Mad Prospect	Mad Tanist
			Caledonian Desire
	Sheila Atlast	The Grand Prince	Champion Prince
			The Grand Duchess
		Last Landing	Man Of Pleasure
			Dannys Gift
CRANOG BET	Knock Hill Chieftain	Galtee Cleo	Sandown Champion
			Cleopatra
		Coolkill Mistress	Celtic Chief
			Coolkill Darkie
	Don't Bet	Glittering Look	Glittering Smack
			Knockrour Favourite
		Don't Ask	Drumman Rambler
			Fawn Queen

Bashful Man
Bk. dog, June '71

MYROSS AGAIN	Knockrour Again	Shaggy Lad	Castledown Lad
			Shaggy Shore
		Buds Bella	Lucky Tanist
			Knockrour Bella
	Bermudas Glory	The Grand Champion	Mad Tanist
			Could Be Worse
		Bermudas Niece	Paving Stone
			Bettys Darling
BALLYFLAKE	Prairie Flash	Hi There	Slaney Record
			Dublin Red
		Prairie Peg	The Grand Champion
			Prairie Vixen
	Here She Comes	Champion Prince	Bellas Prince
			Sallywell
		Raymonds Darling	Sandown Champion
			Big Bawn

Nameless Pixie
Bk. bitch, Jan '77

MONALEE CHAMPION	Crazy Parachute	Hi There	Slaney Record
			Dublin Red
		Mad Prospect	Mad Tanist
			Caledonian Desire
	Sheila Atlast	The Grand Prince	Champion Prince
			The Grand Duchess
		Last Landing	Man Of Pleasure
			Dannys Gift
ITSASTAR	Yanka Boy	Clonalvy Pride	Solar Prince
			Asmena
		Millie Hawthorn	The Grand Fire
			Glittering Millie
	Itsamint	Prairie Flash	Hi There
			Prairie Peg
		Cranog Bet	Knock Hill Chieftain
			Don't Bet

Parkdown Jet
Be. dog, June '79

CAIRNVILLE JET	Own Pride	Always Proud	Clonalvy Pride
			Always A Rebel
		Kitty True	Crazy Parachute
			Ballykinlar Gem
	Cairnville Bet	Monalee Champion	Crazy Parachute
			Sheila Atlast
		Cranog Bct	Knock Hill Chieftain
			Don't Bet
GABRIEL RUBY	Peruvian Style	Kilbelin Style	Prairie Flash
			Clomoney Grand
		Russian Boots	Lucky Wonder
			Shandaroba
	Gabriel Blue	Yanka Boy	Clonalvy Pride
			Millie Hawthorn
		Gabriel Star	The Glen Abbey
			Summerfield Lass

Grove Whisper
F. dog, Feb '85

WHISPER WISHES	Sand Man	Friend Westy	My Friend Lou
			Westy Blubber
		Miss Gorgeous	Tell You Why
			Miss Dilly Mar
	Micklem Drive	Lively Band	Silver Hope
			Kells Queen
		Back O The Gap	Russian Gun
			Poor Linda
GROVE ROAD	Gaily Noble	Monalee Champion	Crazy Parachute
			Sheila Atlast
		Noble Lynn	Flaming King
			Noble Heather
	Overture	Yanka Boy	Clonalvy Pride
			Millie Hawthorn
		Come On Avondhu	Come on Bawnie
			Sixpence

Lartigue Note
Bk. dog, July '87

ONE TO NOTE	Lindas Champion	Monalee Champion	Crazy Parachute
			Sheila Atlast
		Merry Linda	Hack Up Fenian
			Bright Chance
	Hotel Queen	Peruvian Style	Kilbelin Style
			Russian Boots
		Torbal Black	The Grand Silver
			Kitshine
LARTIGUE SPARK	Echo Spark	Liberty Lad	Bright Lad
			Liberty Bell
		Lady Armada	Burgess Heather
			Skipping Chick
	Gabriel Doll	Cairnville Jet	Own Pride
			Cairnville Bet
		Gabriel Ruby	Peruvian Style
			Gabriel Blue

The McKenna Classic Connection

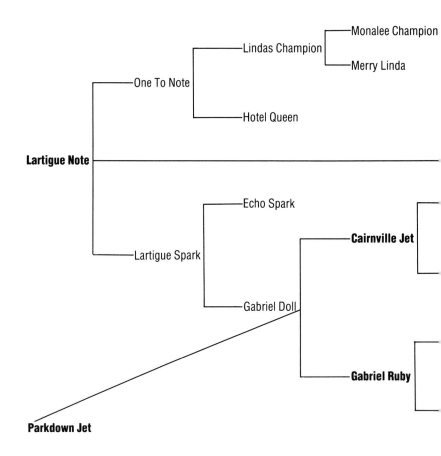

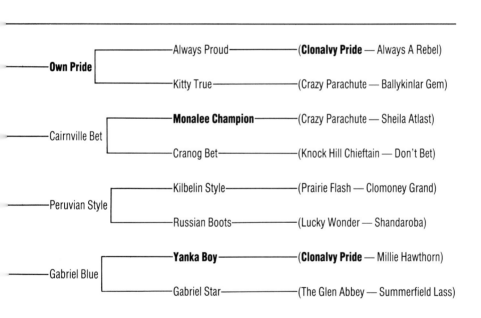

APPENDIX II

Ger McKenna's 32 Classic winners

English Derby (2)

1981 — White City (500m) — Parkdown Jet		29.57
1989 — Wimbledon (480m) — Lartigue Note		28.79

Irish Derby (3)

1969 — Harold's Cross (525y) — Own Pride		29.20
1973 — Shelbourne Park (525y) — Bashful Man		28.82
1987 — Shelbourne Park (550y) — Rathgallen Tady		30.49

Irish Oaks (1)

1979 — Harold's Cross (525y) — Nameless Pixie	29.34

Irish St. Leger (12)
Limerick (550y)

1956 — Prince of Bermuda	30.66	1971 — Time Up Please	30.56
1960 — Swanlands Best	31.60	1972 — Time Up Please	31.05
1962 — Apollo Again	31.26	1975 — Ballybeg Prim	30.44
1965 — Lovely Chieftain	30.92	1976 — Nameless Star	30.62
1967 — Yanka Boy	30.77	1977 — Red Rasper	31.15
1969 — Own Pride	30.95	1984 — Moran's Beef	30.06

Irish Laurels (6)
Cork (525y)

1970 — Gabriel Boy	29.25	1983 — Back Garden	29.66
1976 — Nameless Star	29.30	1984 — Rugged Mick	29.09
1980 — Knockrour Slave	29.00	1985 — Follow A Star	29.42

National Breeders Two-Year-Old Produce Stakes (2)
Clonmel (525y)

1973 — Big Kuda	29.98	1976 — Cill Dubh Darkey	29.64

Irish Cesarewitch (4)
Navan (600y)

1965 — Butterfly Billy	33.26	1975 — Ballybeg Prim	33.30
1967 — Yanka Boy	33.38	1987 — Oughter Brigg	33.08

Irish National Sprint (2)
Dunmore Stadium (435y)

1965 — Bauhus	23.73	1969 — Move Gas	23.60

APPENDIX III
Other Feature Winners
Guinness '600' (3)
Shelbourne Park

1972 — Itsachampion	33.45	1976 — Ballybeg Prim	34.05
1975 — Ballybeg Prim	33.40		

International '525' (4)
Dundalk (525y)

1972 — Time Up Please	29.601973	1979 — Nameless Pixie	29.82
— Bashful Man	29.70	1984 — Rugged Mick	29.34

Irish Puppy Derby (5)
Harold's Cross (525y)

1968 — Always Keen	29.75	1979 — Tivoli Cant	29.88
1974 — Shamrock Point	29.48	1983 — Lauragh Six	29.04
1977 — Hammond	29.46		

Easter Cup (2)
Shelbourne Park (525y)

1969 — Move Gas	30.29	1975 — Tantallon's Flyer	29.60

Tipperary Cup (2)
Thurles (525y — 550y since 1985)

1980 — Carrick Chance	29.50	1982 — Shinrone Jet	29.42

Ger McKenna-trained greyhounds which have won the Bord na gCon National Greyhound Award

1967 — Yanka Boy
1969 — Own Pride
1975 — Ballybeg Prim

1979 — Nameless Pixie
1981 — Parkdown Jet
1984 — Moran's Beef

APPENDIX IV

St Leger Roll of Honour

How a dozen McKenna dogs have dominated the Irish St Leger at Limerick since 1956

1956 — **Prince of Bermuda**	30.66	1973 — Romping to Work	31.04
1957 — Kilcaskin Kern	31.05	1974 — Lively Band	31.20
1958 — Firgrove Snowman	31.28	1975 — **Ballybeg Prim**	30.44
1959 — Ocean Swell	31.18	1976 — **Nameless Star**	30.62
1960 — **Swanlands Best**	31.60	1977 — **Red Rasper**	31.15
1961 — Jerry's Clipper	31.10	1978 — Rhu	31.44
1962 — **Apollo Again**	31.26	1979 — Airmount Champ	31.20
1963 — General Courtnowski	31.12	1980 — Rahan Ship	30.72
1964 — Brook Jockey	31.66	1981 — Oran Jack	30.62
1965 — **Lovely Chieftain**	30.92	1982 — Supreme Tiger	30.44
1966 — Movealong Santa	30.92	1983 — The Stranger	31.04
1967 — **Yanka Boy**	30.77	1984 — **Moran's Beef**	30.06
1968 — Pools Punter	30.88	1985 — Ballintubber One	30.42
1969 — **Own Pride**	30.95	1986 — Storm Villa	30.65
1970 — Mark Anthony	31.02	1987 — Randy	30.23
1971 — **Time Up Please**	30.56	1988 — Local Kate	31.04
1972 — **Time Up Please**	31.05		

APPENDIX V

Irish Derby
Roll of Honour

The McKenna Irish Derby Roll of Honour: How one family left its mark on the premier classic.

★ Joe McKenna.
★★ Tom Lynch.
★★★ Ger McKenna.
★★★★ Gay McKenna.

Year	Winner	Time	Second	Track
1932	Guidless Joe	30.36	Mahloe Man	Shelbourne Park
1933	Monalogue	30.52	Right Incline	Shelbourne Park
1934	Frisco Hobo	30.45	**Buzzing Dick★**	Harold's Cross
1935	Roving Yank	30.18	Roving Spring	Shelbourne Park
1936	Minstrel Rover	30.48	Negro's Equal	Harold's Cross
1937	Muinessa	30.83	Western Skipper	Shelbourne Park
1938	Abbeylara	30.09	Manozzi	Harold's Cross
1939	Marching Thro' Georgia	30.05	Irish Rambler	Limerick
1940	Tanist	29.82	Another Dancing Willie	Shelbourne Park
1941	Brave Damsel	30.64	She's Tidy	Shelbourne Park
1942	Uacterlainn Riac	30.22	Munster Hills	Cork
1943	Famous Knight	30.26	Discretion	Harold's Cross
1944	Clonbonny Bridge	30.53	**Down Signal★★**	Shelbourne Park
1945	Lilac's Luck	30.12	Gun Music	Harold's Cross
1946	Steve	30.20	Manhatten Seale	Shelbourne Park
1947	Daring Flash	30.04	Paddy's Elbow	Harold's Cross
1948	Western Post	29.90	Baytown Colonel	Shelbourne Park

1949	Spanish Lad	29.87	Merry Courier	Harold's Cross
1950	Crossmolina Rambler	29.70	Deep's Dasher	Shelbourne Park
1951	Carmody's Tanist	29.64	**Locht Seal★★**	Harold's Cross
1952	Rough Waters	29.95	Dismal	Shelbourne Park
1953	**Spanish Battleship★★**	29.78	Smokey Glen	Harold's Cross
1954	**Spanish Battleship★★**	29.64	Dignity	Shelbourne Park
1955	**Spanish Battleship★★**	29.53	Crosty's Bell	Harold's Cross
1956	Keep Moving	29.18	**Prince of Bermuda★★★**	Shelbourne Park
1957	Hopeful Cutlet	29.60	The Grand Fire	Harold's Cross
1958	Colonel Perry	29.79	**Daring Customer★★★**	Shelbourne Park
1959	Sir Frederick	29.30	Gallant Winner	Harold's Cross
1960	Perry's Apple	29.55	The Black Ranger	Shelbourne Park
1961	Chieftain's Guest	29.45	**Skip's Choice★★★★**	Harold's Cross
1962	Shane's Legacy	29.58	Golden Cheers	Shelbourne Park
1963	Drumahiskey Venture	29.60	Powerstown Proper	Harold's Cross
1964	Wonder Valley	29.30	Granada Chief	Shelbourne Park
1965	**Ballyowen Chief★★★★**	29.42	Tanyard Heather	Harold's Cross
1966	**Always Proud★★★★**	29.44	**Tiger Chief★★★★**	Shelbourne Park
1967	**Russian Gun★★**	29.44	Dry Flash	Harold's Cross
1968	Yellow Printer	29.11	**Russian Gun★★**	Shelbourne Park
1969	**Own Pride★★★**	29.20	**Monalee Gambler★★**	Harold's Cross
1970	**Monalee Pride★★★★**	29.28	**Own Pride★★★**	Shelbourne Park
1971	Sole Aim	29.12	**Postal Vote★★★★**	Shelbourne Park
1972	**Catsrock Daisy★★★★**	29.20	Waggy Champion	Shelbourne Park
1973	**Bashful Man★★★**	28.82	**Rita's Choice★★★★**	Shelbourne Park
1974	Lively Band	29.11	Wind Jammer	Shelbourne Park
1975	Shifting Shadow	29.35	Moonshine Bandit	Shelbourne Park

1976	Tain Mor	29.35	Carn Top	Shelbourne Park
1977	Linda's Champion	29.53	Brush Tim	Shelbourne Park
1978	Pampered Rover	29.23	**Here's Tat***★★★	Shelbourne Park
1979	Penny County	29.28	Distant Clamour	Shelbourne Park
1980	Suir Miller	29.18	Another Trail	Shelbourne Park
1981	Bold Work	29.32	Calandra Champ	Shelbourne Park
1982	Coolaine Super	29.34	Milwaukee Prince	Shelbourne Park
1983	Belvedere Bran	29.65	**Brideview Sailor***★★★	Shelbourne Park
1984	Dipmac	29.15	Glencorbry Celt	Shelbourne Park
1985	Tubbercurry Lad	29.14	Manorville Sand	Shelbourne Park
1986	Kyle Jack	30.41	Murlen's Slippy	Shelbourne Park
1987	**Rathgallen Tady***★★★	30.49	Carter's Lad	Shelbourne Park
1988	Make History	30.26	Manorville Magic	Shelbourne Park
1989	Manorville Magic	30.53	Mac's Lock	Shelbourne Park

(Irish Derby sponsored by P.J. Carroll and Co. 1970–87; Kerry Group PLC 1988–)

Run continuously at Shelbourne Park since 1970.

Run over 525 yards from 1932–85; 550 yards from 1986–

APPENDIX VI

Mckenna's Great Greyhounds

Date of Whelping

August 1953 — Prince of Bermuda.
bd.d. (Champion Prince — Sunora).
Bred: Denis O'Shea, Borrisoleigh, Co. Tipperary.
Owned: Mrs Elizabeth Buckley, Nenagh, Co. Tipperary.
1956 — Won — Irish St Leger, Limerick, 550 yards (30.66).
    Ran 28.98 heat of Irish Derby becoming first
    greyhound to break 29 seconds, Shelbourne Park,
    525 yards.
    Runner-up — Irish Derby, Shelbourne Park, 525 yards.
    Ran 27.95 heat Irish Laurels, Cork, 500 yards. Track
    record which still stands.
    Runner-up — Irish Laurels, Cork, 500 yards.
April 1958 — Swanlands Best.
bd.d. (Man of Pleasure — Swanland Neighbour).
Bred: John Buckley, Emly, Co. Tipperary.
Owned: John O'Dwyer and Mrs John Delahunty, Thurles, Co.
Tipperary.
1960 — Won — Irish St Leger, Limerick, 550 yards, (31.60).
November 1959 — Apollo Again.
bd.d. (Knockrour Again — Redondo Beach).
Bred: Patrick Collins, Knocknagoshel, Co. Kerry.
Owned: Patrick Grace, Pallasgreen, Co. Limerick.
1962 — Won — Irish St Leger, Limerick, 550 yards, (31.26).
October 1962 — Bauhus.
fw.d. (Solar Prince — Lovely Sister).

Bred: Patrick Hogan, Pallasgreen, Co. Limerick.

Owned: Pat Dalton, Golden, Co. Tipperary.

1965 — Won — Irish National Sprint, Dunmore Stadium 435 yards, (23.73).

August 1963 — Lovely Chieftain.

f.d. (Knock Hill Chieftain — Lovely Sister).

Bred: Patrick Hogan, Pallasgreen, Co. Limerick.

Owned: Pat Dalton, Golden, Co. Tipperary (later Mrs Josie McKenna, Borrisokane, Co. Tipperary).

1965 — Won — Irish St Leger, Limerick, 550 yards (30.92).

September 1963 — Butterfly Billy.

wbk.d. (Pigalle Wonder — Eight Spot).

Bred and Owned: Michael Riordan, Buttevant, Co. Cork.

1965 — Won — Irish Cesarewitch, Navan 600 yards, (33.26).

Ran 33.61, Mullingar 600 yards. Time still stands as track record.

June 1964 — Move Handy.

bd.d. (Dandy Man — Move Sally).

Bred and owned: Martin Hogan, Cloughjordan, Co. Tipperary.

March 1965 — Yanka Boy.

f.d. (Clonalvy Pride — Millie Hawthorn).

Bred: Patsy Richardson, Doon, Co. Limerick.

Owned: Mick Loughnane, Roscrea, Co. Tipperary (later Eamonn O'Reilly and Sean Leahy, Loughrea, Co. Galway).

1967 — Won — Irish St Leger, Limerick, 550 yards (30.77).

Won — Irish Cesarewitch, Navan, 600 yards (33.38).

Won — Midland Puppy Stake, Mullingar, 525 yards (30.46) Irish Greyhound of the Year 1967.

June 1965 — Proud Lincoln.

fw.d. (Clonalvy Pride — Gettysburg Princess).

Bred: James Delargey, Antrim.

Owned: A.S. Lucas, Bray, Co. Wicklow (later Mrs Josie McKenna, Borrisokane, Co. Tipperary).

July 1965 — Proud Choice.

bd.d. (Clonalvy Pride — Blacknose Trixie).

Bred and Owned: A.S. Lucas, Bray, Co. Wicklow.

April 1966 — Irish Rain.

bd.d. (Wonder Valley — Sonny's Gift).

Bred: Daniel J. Cronin, Newmarket, Co. Cork.

Owned: Martin Divilly, Galway; and Joseph D. Coyle, Lurgan, Co. Armagh.

May 1967 — Own Pride.

bd.d (Always Proud — Kitty True).

Bred: Ignatius Kelly, Cooraclare, Co. Clare.

Owned: Thomas O'Doherty, Cree, Co. Clare.

1969 — Won — Irish St Leger, Limerick, 550 yards (30.95).
       Won — Irish Derby, Harold's Cross, 525 yards (29.20).
       Irish Greyhound of the Year 1969.

1970 — Runner-up — Irish Derby, Shelbourne Park, 525 yards.

June 1967 — Move Gas.

f.d. (Dandy Man — Move Sally).

Bred: Martin Hogan, Cloughjordan, Co. Tipperary.

Owned: Richard Liffey, Birr, Co. Offaly) (later Edward Farnham, Keady, Co. Armagh).

1969 — Won — Easter Cup, Shelbourne Park, 525 yards (30.29).
       Won — Irish National Sprint, Dunmore Stadium, 435 yards
       (23.60).

August 1968 — Gabriel Boy.

Be.bd. d. (Yanka Boy — Gabriel Star).

Bred: William Shannon, Balldehob, Co. Cork.

Owned: Pat Dalton, Golden, Co. Tipperary.

1970 — Won — Irish Laurels, Cork, 525 yards (29.25).

June 1969 — Time Up Please.

bk.d. (Newdown Heather — Dogstown Fame).

Bred: Patsy Browne, Kells, Co. Kilkenny).

Owned: Mick Loughnane, Roscrea, Co. Tipperary (later Mr J. Loughnane, Dublin), (later C.A. Murphy, Nova Scotia, Canada).

1971 — Won — Irish St. Leger, Limerick, 550 yards (30.56).

1972 — Won — Irish St Leger, Limerick, 550 yards (31.05).
       Won — International '525', Dundalk (29.60).

June 1969 — Ballykilty.

wbd.d. (Always Proud — Kitty True).

Bred: Ignatius Kelly, Cooraclare, Co. Clare.

Owned: Eamonn Gaynor, Quin, Co. Clare (later Conor Hynes, Portumna, Co. Galway).

1971 — Ran 28.80 heat Irish Derby, Shelbourne Park.

November 1970 — Itsachampion.
bk.d. (Monalee Champion — Cranog Bet).
Bred: William L. McNair, Newtownards, Co. Down.
Owned: Miss Deirdre Hynes, Portumna, Co. Galway.
Won — Guinness 600, Shelbourne Park (33.45).
January 1971 — Big Kuda.
bd.d. (Kilbeg Kuda — Far Down).
Bred: Miss Elieen Kirwan, Glenmore, Co. Kilkenny.
Owned: Thomas Duggan and Stephen Power, Glenmore, Co.
Kilkenny.
1973 — Won — National Breeders Two-Year-Old Produce Stakes,
            Clonmel, 525 yards (29.98).
        Won — Munster Puppy Cup, Clonmel, 525 yards (30.08).
May 1971 — Ballymaclune.
bd.d. (Yanka Boy — Kitty True).
Bred: Ignatius Kelly, Cooraclare, Co. Clare.
Owned: Eamonn Gaynor, Quin, Co. Clare.
1974 — Runner up — Irish Laurels, Cork, 525 yards.
        Won — Guinness Trophy, Cork, 525 yards (29.50).
May 1971 — Ballyroughan.
wbk.d. (Yanka Boy — Kitty True).
Bred: Ignatius Kelly, Cooraclare, Co. Clare.
Owned: Eamonn Gaynor, Quin, Co. Clare.
June 1971 — Bashful Man.
bk.d. (Myross Again — Ballyflake).
Bred: Mrs Nancy Birrane, Kilmallock, Co. Limerick.
Owned: Miss Deirdre Hynes, Portumna, Co. Galway.
1973 — Won — Irish Derby, Shelbourne Park, 525 yards (28.82).
                Fastest time ever in Irish Derby final.
        Won — International 525, Dundalk (29.70).
January 1973 — Shamrock Point.
wbk.d. (Monalee Champion — Gruelling Point).
Bred: Fintan Hall, Mullinahone, Co. Tipperary.
Owned: Joseph O'Connor, Cahir, Co. Tipperary.
1974 — Won — Irish Puppy Derby, Harold's Cross, 525 yards
            (29.48).
March 1973 — Ballybeg Prim.
f.d. (Rockfield Era — Ballybeg Pride).

Bred: John Brennan and Phil McGovern, Thurles, Co. Tipperary.
Owned: John Bullen, Lincolnshire (later Grovenor Cleaning Services, Belfast).
1975 — Won — Irish St Leger, Limerick, 550 yards (30.44).
       Won — Irish Cesarewitch, Navan, 600 yards (33.30).
       Won — Guinness 600, Shelbourne Park (33.40).
       Irish Greyhound of the Year 1975.
1976 — Won — Guinness 600, Shelbourne Park (33.40).
       Runner-up — English Derby, White City, 500m.

February 1974 — Cill Dubh Darkey.
bk.d. (Mortar Light — Cill Dubh Lane).
Bred and Owned: Michael Bergin (Snr), Freshford, Co. Kilkenny.
1976 — Won — National Breeders Two-Year-Old Produce Stakes, Clonmel, 525 (29.64).

May 1974 — Nameless Star.
f.d. (Rita's Choice — Itsastar).
Bred: John B. McCauley, Shankill, Co. Dublin.
Owned: Mrs Rita McAuley, Shankill, Co. Dublin (later Grovenor Cleaning Services, Belfast).
1976 — Won — Irish Laurels, Cork, 525 yards (29.30).
       Won — Irish St Leger, Limerick, 550 yards (30.62).

June 1975 — Red Rasper.
bd.d. (Own Pride — Miss Honeygar).
Bred: William O'Donoghue, Bruff, Co. Limerick.
Owned: John Bullen, Lincolnshire.
1977 — Won — Irish St Leger, Limerick, 550 yards (31.15).

April 1976 — Sweeping Bally.
f.b. (Ballymaclune — Sweeping Brush).
Bred: J.P. Ryan, Knocklong, Co. Limerick.
Owned: Ger McKenna, Borrisokane, Co. Tipperary.

April 1977 — Knockrour Slave.
wbk. d. (Sole Aim — Knockrour Exile).
Bred: Andy Lynch, Cappoquin, Co. Waterford.
Owned: Noel Lynch, Aughabullogue, Co. Cork.
1980 — Won — Irish Laurels, Cork, 525 yards (29.00).

July 1977 — Nameless Pixie.
bk.b. (Monalee Champion — Itsastar).
Bred: John B. McAuley, Shankill, Co. Dublin.

Owned: Mrs Rita McAuley, Shankill. Co. Dublin.

1979 — Won — Irish Oaks, Harold's Cross, 525 yards (29.34).

Won — International 525, Dundalk (29.82).

Irish Greyhound of the Year 1979.

June 1979 — Parkdown Jet.

be.d. (Cairnville Jet — Gabriel Ruby).

Bred: William Shannon, Ballydehob, Co. Cork.

Owned: Sean Barnett and Robert Shannon, Schull, Co. Cork.

1981 — Won — English Derby, White City, 500m (29.57).

Irish Greyhound of the Year 1981.

August 1980 — Ramtogue Champ.

bd.d. (Witches Champion — Rushin Out).

Bred: Patrick McKeon, Galway.

Owned: Mrs Elizabeth Furlong, Ballybrack, Co. Dublin.

May 1981 — Count Five.

f.d. (Sail On — All Jam).

Bred: Andrew Hickey, Cashel, Co. Tipperary.

Owned: Cathal McCarthy, Ballybay, Co. Monaghan (later Mrs Joan Ferris, Bansha, Co. Tipperary).

1984 — Ran 28.95 semi-finals Irish Derby, Shelbourne Park, 525 yards.

July 1981 — Back Garden.

bk.d. (Knockrour Slave — Sweeping Bally).

Bred: Ger McKenna, Borrisokane, Co. Tipperary.

Owned: Eamonn McLoughney, Nenagh, Co. Tipperary (later Noel J. Loughran and Cathal Horan, Tralee, Co. Kerry).

1983 — Won — Irish Laurels, Cork 525 yards, (29.66).

Won — Anglo-Irish International, Shelbourne Park, 525 yards (29.37).

1984 — Runner-up — Irish Laurels, Cork 525 yards .

September 1981 — Lauragh Six.

bk.d. (Garradrimna — Emmerdale Pride).

Bred: Liam Jones, Listowel, Co. Kerry.

Owned: Tony Brennan, Castlemartyr, Co. Cork (later Denis McCarthy, Mallow, Co. Cork).

1983 — Won — Irish Puppy Derby, Harold's Cross, 525 yards (29.04).

Ran 19.33 Shelbourne Park, 360 yards.

Time still stands as track record.
Ran 28.96 Cork, 525 yards.

November 1981 — Rugged Mick.
bd.d. (Ceili Band — Blueberry Pet).
Bred: Christy Hayes, Hospital, Co. Limerick.
Owned: Pat Murphy, Belfast (later Carl van Waltleben, London).
1984 — Won — Irish Laurels, Cork, 525 yards (29.09).
  Won — International 525, Dundalk (29.34).

March 1982 — Moran's Beef.
bd.d. (Nobel Brigg — Rathkenny Bride).
Bred: William Leahy, Abbeydorney, Co. Kerry.
Owned: Tony Brennan, Castlemartyr, Co. Cork.
1984 — Runner-up — English Derby, White City, 500m.
  Won — Irish St Leger, Limerick, 550 yards (30.06). The
    time still stands as track record.
  Won — Anglo-Irish International, Shelbourne Park, 525
    yards (29.39).
  Irish Greyhound of the Year 1984.

June 1983 — Follow A Star.
f.d. (Under Par — Float A Loan).
Bred: Donal Desmond, Lombardstown, Co. Cork.
Owned: Denis Murphy, Whitechurch, Co. Cork.
1985 — Won — Irish Laurels, Cork 525 yards, (29.42).

September 1983 — Here's Negrow.
bk.d. (Sand Man — Here's Jenny).
Bred: Ms Kitty Skehan, Johnstown, Co. Kilkenny.
Owned: Tony Mulgrew, Cookstown, Co. Tyrone.

May 1984 — Master Mystery (late Moon River).
bd.d. (Ballyheigue Moon — Susie's Liberator).
Bred: Patrick Mulcahy, Tournafulla, Co. Limerick.
Owned: John Doherty, Tournafulla, Co. Limerick.
1986 — Won — Champion Stakes, Shelbourne Park, 575 yards
  (32.00).

July 1984 — Oughter Brigg.
f.d. (Noble Brigg — Dromacossane).
Bred: James J. Boyle, Tralee, Co. Kerry).
Owned: Maurice McEllistrim, Tralee, Co. Kerry.
1987 — Won — Irish Cesarewitch, Navan, 600 yards (33.08).

February 1985 — Grove Whisper.

f.d. (Whisper Wishes — Grove Road).

Bred: Sean McCarthy, Mallow, Co. Cork.

Owned: Tony Brennan, Castlemartyr, Co. Cork.

1987 — Won — Anglo-Irish International, Shelbourne Park, 550
            yards (30.43).

    Won — Kennedy Cup, Limerick, 525 yards (29.15).

    Won — Paddy Stakes, Youghal, 550 yards (30.58).

July 1985 — Lundy's Call.

f.d. (Echo Spark — Silver Lundy).

Bred: Michael O'Toole, Charletille, Co. Cork.

Owned: Patsy Byrne, Surrey (later Bill Gaskin, Suffolk).

October 1985 — Rathgallen Tady.

bd.d. (Overdraught Pet — Mea West).

Bred: Colm McCarthy, Cashel, Co. Tipperary).

Owned: Eddie Costello, Middlesex (later John T. Meadham, Victoria,
Australia).

1987 — Won — Irish Derby, Shelbourne Park, 550 yards (30.49).

May 1986 — Bold Rabbit.

bk.d. (Whisper Wishes — Contact Breaker).

Bred: Patsy Byrne, Surrey.

Owned: Patsy Byrne, Surrey.

July 1987 — Lartigue Note.

bk. d. (One To Note — Lartigue Spark).

Bred: Mrs Mary Moore, Ballybunion, Co. Kerry).

Owned: Cathal McCarthy, Ballybay, Co. Monaghan.

1989 — Won — English Derby, Wimbledon, 480m (28.79).

Bibliography

Blanning, Charles, and Prescott, Sir Mark: The Waterloo Cup — The First 150 Years (Heath House Press).

Clarke, H. Edward: The Greyhound (Popular Dogs).

Comyn, John (ed.): Trap To Line (Aherlow Ltd.).

Fortune, Michael: Irish Greyhound Derby (Victory Irish Promotions).

Fortune, Michael (ed.): Irish Greyhound Review, Vols 1–11 (Victory Irish Promotions).

Genders, Roy: The Encylopaedia of Greyhound Racing (Pelham).

Lennox, Alan: Guide To Good Stud Dogs (Greyhound Magazine Co. Ltd.).

Murphy, Jack: Never Venture — Never Win (Business and Shopping Guide Ltd.).